GOOD WORK

RECLAIMING YOUR INNER AMBITION

PAUL MILLERD

PATHLESS
PUBLISHING

Paperback ISBN: 979-8-9855153-8-1

Hardcover ISBN: 978-1-965701-02-7

PDF ISBN: 979-8-9855153-9-8

EPUB ISBN: 979-8-9855153-7-4

Kindle ISBN: 978-1-965701-00-3

iBook ISBN: 978-1-965701-01-0

Editing and book coaching by Paula Trucks-Pape. Cover design by Tianna Solomon. Illustrations by Melina Burhan.

To Angie and Michelle

CONTENTS

INTRODUCTION

Could it be this simple? Just do things you like?

Sitting there at the table in my Airbnb in Taipei, a cup of coffee by my side, I felt that my reality had shifted.

It all started to make sense: the endless job-hopping in my twenties, the dissatisfaction that never seemed to go away, the desire to escape to Asia after quitting my job and blowing up my life. The whole time, I had been desperately searching for something I could never quite understand, and now I had found it.

"How could I have missed it?" I thought. For years I had written for fun and always found so much joy in it. Since I had quit my job sixteen months earlier, writing had been my only consistent activity. But I never considered it "work." At 33 years old, I finally realized that this act of creative expression was an essential part of me.

It was my good work.

I stopped writing, took a deep breath and took in my

surroundings. Rain pattered down on the metal awnings of the buildings on the street. The air in the room was heavy and humid and carried a musty scent from the wooden furniture that had likely been passed down from previous generations. In a city where most cafés don't open until 11am, my pot of freshly brewed coffee filled the air with a distinctly American urgency I had yet to let go of.

Since I had arrived in the apartment a few weeks earlier, this table had been my sanctuary. Each morning, I would make coffee, sit down, and write. But on this particular morning, I had a profound awakening. Channeling my curiosity into a newsletter post destined for just a small number of readers, I noticed a deep connection with my work, hyper-aware of it for the first time. I felt at ease, filled with a sense of abundance and possibility.

The moment was a stark contrast to my life up until that point. For ten years I had bounced from job to job, searching for a sense of connection to my work that remained elusive, and by the end I simply ran out of energy to keep going. Pinpointing the exact cause of my burnout is an impossible task. It may have been the meetings where everyone only pretended to care, or how emails from clients were treated as secret messages to be decoded as the team jumped into crisis mode. Maybe it was simply knowing that I was playing a role in the whole performance, turning myself into the kind of person who gets a good review and a 5% raise at the end of the year.

A perfect explanation doesn't really matter because by the end, I was depleted. Despite having what was, on paper, a promising career, I saw no reasonable path forward. When I quit, it wasn't an act of defiance but surrender. I had been vanquished by the demands of a modern career and as I walked away, I saw work itself as my unofficial adversary. *It had done this to me.*

With this mindset, I had no bold visions of success when I became self-employed. I wasn't taking a leap to build a successful startup or even trying to increase my earnings. Quite the opposite. I saw work as something I needed to escape and my plan was to eliminate as much of it from my life as possible. I'd live simply and scrape by.

As I cut my cost of living in that first year, I had the thrilling sensation of becoming free. *Wow! It was working.* I was doing the bare minimum to pay the bills and I felt better.

I thought I had it all figured out, but I was only getting started. Without "work," I spent more time doing things I enjoyed, like writing. No matter where I was I kept finding myself lost in flow, typing away, trying to find a rhythm with my words. But it was not until sitting at that table in Taipei that I saw it for what it was: work worth doing. I didn't want to escape work; I just craved work I cared about.

In seeking to break free from work, I rediscovered it

in a simpler and more powerful form. I realized that my conception of "work" had been far too narrow.

As I awakened to this new perspective, I became upset:

Why didn't anyone tell me that this is possible?!

Why do so many of us pretend that formatting Power-Point slides is the height of human existence? That jobs are the only form of work?

I loved the feeling of connection and flow I experienced from writing and it became everything to me. I became determined to build my life around doing things like writing. Things that mattered to me. Things that brought me alive. No matter what.

Despite not having earned any money in months, and with no evidence that this ill-formed approach to life was sensible, I fully committed to this new direction.

But the changes I started making as I continued down this new path were hard for me to understand and even more incomprehensible to others:

"What's your plan?"

"I don't know, I feel like I'm on to something though."

"What do you do all day?"

"Um, well, I just sort of see where my interests take me. Most days, I wake up and find myself writing."

"Are you trying to get paid for that?"

"No."

"Aren't you worried about the future? What about making money? Are you going to get another job?"

"If I can help it, I'll never get another job. I like what I'm doing, I just want to see where it leads."

"You are crazy."

"Thank you."

I was embracing what I eventually started calling my pathless path, which did not come with any semblance of a plan. This is the challenge of good work: searching for it might lead you away from what others view as "success," and it might even lead you to question your own sanity. For me, however, the resulting transformation has been worth it. For too long, I had embraced a shallow version of life, seeing work as a means to an end, as a pursuit of goals that were supposed to make me happy.

Through writing, I started to find what I truly craved, and as a result, I completely lost interest in the outcomes of my work, namely making money and external achievements. Writing was a refuge, a place where I could transcend feeling lost in my life. It was enough. So I designed my entire life around creating the time and space to think, wander, and write. Nothing else mattered. And for the next few years, I committed myself to this path, putting creative work, especially writing, above all else. To get by, I experimented with all kinds of gig work, doing my best to find things that paid the bills without draining my energy or time. If I achieved any kind of financial success, I wanted it to result *only* from a life centered around good work.

Now, six years after committing to writing, and seven

years after quitting my job, I am far wealthier in terms of time, freedom, and a sense of agency in my life. Here's the crazy thing too: my good work has started to generate *some* money. In the last few years, I've sold more than 50,000 copies of my first book, *The Pathless Path,* generating more than $200,000 in profits. This resulted directly from my commitment to good work.

Which is wild.

Does this mean good work can make you a lot of money? I can't promise that. In fact, the idea that you *should* be able to make money from your passions is a story that holds too many people back from finding good work. Personally, I've sacrificed hundreds of thousands of dollars in income to pursue this path, something which will make more sense after you read Chapter 12.

In writing this second book, I'm again choosing to spend most of my time doing something that's not guaranteed to make money. This decision was easy, however, because writing a book involves channeling my inner ambition, the deepest expression of what I want out of life. At the beginning of my career, this inner fire drove me to pursue impressive achievements. But over time, that flame faded, and I almost forgot it existed. By embarking on a pathless path, I've rekindled that flame, which guides me not toward societal benchmarks of success, but toward a life centered around good work. Through the connection to my work, I feel fully alive, able to show up as the boldest expression of who I want to be. On this path, I can channel my ambition beyond life as only a successful worker, showing up as a fully present and connected father, spouse, and friend.

This inner drive has pulled me through writing this book as I manage the hard constraints of being a parent. I've adapted my writing process to fit my life, writing in three hour blocks at cafés, sometimes with fellow writer friends, and sneaking more time when my daughter Michelle is asleep. At the end of each week I feel content and fulfilled. In my twenties, I never felt this way. I wasted my time doing work of little consequence. Now, after experiencing the nourishing feeling of doing work that matters to me, I'm willing to do almost anything to continue to live this way. As long as I have some buffer in savings to keep going, I will.

Good work is powerful. It can reshape what you desire from life. It can fill your days with a renewable form of life energy that you want to protect. Nevertheless, good work is hard to define, which makes it difficult to explain. Good work is often tied to a certain activity or combination of activities that you don't want to skip. Throughout my life, my good work will likely consist of many activities I enjoy, like writing, teaching, mentoring others, and even being a father. Right now, writing is the core activity, and it includes many kinds of expressions, such as essays, videos, and books.

Your good work may shift over time. For example, it may primarily help you find fulfillment or let you express your creativity, while at other times it may help you make money. Sometimes it may completely absorb you, while during other periods, you may struggle to stay connected to it. Good work doesn't usually happen on a factory schedule and often has a natural seasonality. But when you stop doing it, good work seduces you back. It is something you must do. Once you discover your good work, take it seriously and protect it, as it can be one of the most powerful ways to show up in the world, contribute, and feel useful.

When I quit my job I did not understand any of this. I assumed I would still have to orient my life around work I didn't enjoy. I was stunned when I discovered activities that didn't require me to grind, desperate to hit the bar every Friday.

It's clear now: work doesn't have to suck.

I wrote this book to show you that this is possible and to help you reflect on your own path and figure out what "good work" means for you. But you won't find a simple framework or step-by-step playbook here. The reality is that good work is simple, but hard: it requires self-reflection, trial and error, and having faith in yourself and the world. My journey has taken years and is still evolving. I've had to mourn the loss of parts of myself that once served me, while also reconnecting with other parts of myself that I had suppressed. Going through this experience has tested me, but given me strength. It filled me with an inner confidence that helped me rewrite my own story, not as someone who "wasted" my career by walking away, but as someone doing something far more ambitious. Most importantly, this path allows me to openly admit that I care about what I do, without shame or cynicism – something I couldn't do in my former career.

That day in Taipei, I didn't just aim my life in a new direction – I took the first steps toward reclaiming my raw, inner ambition. It was a powerful moment, but it was also only the start. In Bali, several months later, I would be tested and need to reaffirm my commitment. Afterward, I would still spend the next few years learning to coexist with my own doubts and fears.

Now, I'm able to look back more clearly at all the challenges I've faced and see how I was able to keep going. It was only through this strange, confusing, and meandering journey that I have been able to find myself on a path where I genuinely feel like I'm thriving. How long can I keep this going? I can't tell you that. But for now, I've made it work for almost six years, and for me, that means it *can* work. That's enough.

I wrote this book to show you that reclaiming your inner ambition and finding good work is not only possible, but worth pursuing. It's also my attempt to inject you with the pragmatic optimism that is necessary in a world filled with cynicism and doom, particularly about work.

It's never too late to start looking for your good work. I didn't discover mine until my mid-thirties, but once I did, it sparked a transformation in every aspect of my life. The journey will be uniquely yours, filled with challenges and unexpected breakthroughs. My aspiration is that you consider this book your friendly companion as you step onto this path. May it help you rediscover your inner fire and craft a life around work that truly matters to you.

PART ONE
AWAKEN TO
GOOD WORK

"Before you tell your life what you intend to do with it, listen for what it intends to do with you. Before you tell your life what truths and values you have decided to live up to, let your life tell you what truths you embody, what values you represent."[1]

— PARKER PALMER

"I don't know where I'm going, but I know exactly how to get there."[2]

— BOYD VARTY

"Finding good work and doing good work is one of the ultimate ways of making a break for freedom."[3]

— DAVID WHYTE

1

EMBRACE THE UNKNOWN

Sixteen months before moving to Taiwan, I quit my consulting job. The first few months were not an awakening, but simply about survival. In theory, I was free. I had taken my heroic leap, ridding myself of the burdens of corporate life. But all I could think about was my lack of an income. I thought finding a few consulting projects could solve the problem and, for a while, it did. Earning those first dollars on my own gave me a powerful sense of agency and convinced me I wouldn't go broke. Nine months into self-employment, I had landed four different projects and proved to myself that I could "make it" working on my own. But I had a problem: those projects were the same kind I had done in my consulting career, and as my financial anxiety diminished, I discovered that I didn't actually want to build a life around this kind of work.

When I was working in consulting, I simply

completed my tasks, driven by peer pressure to be a "good worker" and meet my team's expectations. I never thought too deeply about my interest in the work. After all, I had little choice. When I started working on my own, however, tasks that used to be easy to finish suddenly felt impossible. For one of my freelance projects, I had to send an update email to the client before a check-in call on Friday. I showed up at the coworking center I had joined in Boston that Monday intending to complete it. I knew it wouldn't take me more than fifteen minutes. But I spent the entire day procrastinating, working on other things that interested me, wandering back and forth to the coffee and snacks area, and taking a long bike ride around the river. As I left for the day, I swore to myself, "*Tomorrow I'll do it.*" But then Tuesday came and went and so did Wednesday. The task hung over me all week until I forced myself to do it at the end of the day on Thursday. Hitting "Send," I knew deep in my body that I couldn't keep going like this.

This realization hit me hard; not only did I have to face the fact that I had spent most of my days doing tasks like this in my career, I also had no real plan for supporting myself other than doing this same kind of work, now as a freelancer. But the longer I spent away from my former job, the more certain I was that consulting was probably never the work I was meant to be doing. Consulting projects could earn me money, but

I saw them as a trap. *What was the point of quitting if I was just going to recreate my former life?*

Instead of tackling another project, I needed time to figure things out, and that meant lowering my cost of living. I had already gotten my rent down to $800 a month in Boston. The next step was to cancel my coworking membership, lowering my monthly costs by $450. With a lower burn, I felt less pressure and "bought" myself time to think.

Part of the reason I felt comfortable with this shift was the sense of aliveness that was sneaking into my life. As the consulting projects wound down, I would wake up each morning with an explosive energy, drawn to creative projects and other experiments. I moved my writing on Medium to a personal blog called *Boundless*. I began regularly writing and sending a newsletter about my interests, something I'm still writing to this day. I also decided to launch a podcast, and despite feeling terrified about interviewing people, I sent out my first invites.

At the same time, I stopped looking for consulting projects and sought out news kinds of work. I pitched a local startup about helping them with a report on the future of work and landed my first paid writing project. Despite only earning $1,000 for close to a hundred hours of work, I enjoyed it, and the team was so impressed they invited me to an all-inclusive paid trip to Dallas for a conference. Another gig I pursued was being a Teacher's Assistant for a summer class at MIT. One of my favorite

professors, Professor Hafrey, had taken over the leader-
ship curriculum for the program I had graduated from. I
pitched him on helping with the class. He loved the idea
of having an alumnus in the classroom. I earned a small
stipend, and was energized by being on campus, but more
importantly, I tested out what it felt like to "work" in a
different kind of way. Around the same time, I also
launched a small online course called "Solopreneur Shift"
and persuaded eight people to join one of my first experiments in making money through my own creations. Even
though I wasn't making much money from these projects,
every day I woke up filled with excitement. I was doing
things that I enjoyed, and while I had glimpsed this state
in the previous few years, it now began to fill my days.

I noticed this aliveness beyond my work, too, in the
small laughs that bubbled up on bike rides and walks
through many of Boston's neighborhoods. One day, as a
friend and I strolled through the Boston Public Garden,
she pointed out dozens of exotic trees from around the
world. There were trees from Japan, Norway, and many
other countries. *What?!* I was shocked. For ten years, I
had biked and walked through the park, sat with friends
on the grass, and people watched on park benches. But I
had never *really* seen it.

I thought, *"What else am I missing?"*
What else is there to discover that is right in front of me?

I wanted to stay connected to this expanded awareness and see where it took me. Despite my determination, though, it would slip away when I found myself

amidst the towering buildings where I used to work, or on the train, shoulder to shoulder with swarms of anxious professionals, or in conversations with people triggered by my lack of a plan. I was filled with the dual sense of wanting to run away while excitedly reaching toward a more promising future, one that I couldn't see.

To deal with this tension, I reflexively rejected everything from my former life and started doing the opposite. Before, I always had a plan. Now, I distrusted plans. I knew I *should* think about making money and landing clients, but I was more drawn to the question, *What if I do literally anything else other than work for money?* To the people around me, I appeared reckless, and to some degree they were right. A certain amount of destruction is inevitable during a life transition. But even without a plan, I felt a deeper source of wisdom inside of me.

One of my good friends, Erv, had quit his job a couple years earlier and had traveled the world for a year before settling in Taiwan to teach English and study Chinese. He seemed to be enjoying his new path and whenever I thought about him, I felt so inspired. Walking around in Boston, he popped into my head and without thinking, I texted him, "I'm thinking of doing a trip to Asia, should I visit you in Taiwan in April?"

The trip made no sense financially: I had no paid work in the pipeline and hadn't been searching for any. But as my days became more filled with creativity and self-directed projects, I felt pulled toward the unknown. I began trusting that things would work out anyway and I realized how much my previous, highly planned approach undermined opportunities for serendipity and adventure. Watching my bank balance shrink in the months before the trip and not doing anything about it constituted a quiet rebellion. I was happily creating space for the new energy unfolding in my life.

When I arrived in Taiwan, the aliveness I had started to feel in Boston was amplified. Trying new food at the Raohe night market, biking along the river on the edge of Taipei, riding scooters along the cliffs in Hualien, hiking in Taroko national park, and taking in the Taipei landscape atop Elephant Mountain all filled me with wonder. At the end of the week, I told Erv I was going to find a way to come back.

Because I had spent almost my entire life in the northeastern U.S., the idea of moving to Taiwan felt radical. When I arrived back in Boston, I remember telling one of my close friends about my plan and feeling a visceral sense of shame in my body as I voiced my intentions. His reaction shocked me: "Cool!" I had expected him to criticize the plan. This intrigued me. *Why was I so scared to do something like this? Why did it feel so shameful?* With each person I told, these powerful stories about what I "should" be doing loosened their grip, and it felt like I was softening into a new version of myself, one that felt natural and right.

Eventually I bought a flight ticket, ended my lease, and started getting rid of my possessions. Many people have a deep desire to do the same: get rid of everything and start fresh. It's exactly what I did and I am happy to report that it feels as good as you would expect. To others, it looked like I was blowing up my life, but I felt like I was kicking off a grand adventure. When people asked me what I was doing, I didn't have an answer, but for the first time in my life, I was comfortable with that.

The night before I flew back to Taipei, I stayed with a friend working in finance in New York City. Sitting in his tiny living room, we caught up on our lives. He was filled with excitement, having recently landed a job at his dream company in private equity. I loved seeing him like that. It made me think back to early in my career when I broke into consulting, against the odds. But now, as I sat there, struggling to explain what I was doing, the world of conventional careers felt so distant.

The next day, I boarded the train, heading to the airport. During the hour-long ride, I was still filled with an intense feeling of guilt, as if I was doing something wrong. *Why wasn't I completely excited about this adventure?* This feeling stayed with me until I boarded the plane. As I sat there, about to take off from New York, excitement started to show up. I was thrilled to step into this new chapter of my life, but at the same time I also started to feel the subtle pangs of grief that come from letting go of an important part of yourself. As the plane flew into the vast expanse of the sky over the Atlantic Ocean, I knew there was no going back. I was leaving behind my home and my identity as an achiever, a safe refuge which had gotten me to this point but was no longer serving me. I was stepping into the unknown, my future a mystery waiting to be discovered.

Upon arrival in Taiwan, I had no specific plans beyond a tentative flight to Vietnam two months later. But each day, as I rose from the small twin bed in my Airbnb, I would find myself drawn to the small communal table where I would open my laptop and write. Often Yogee, my host, would be starting his day too. I would nod and say "Zao An," (早安) or "Good morning" in Chinese, one of the few phrases I had just learned. We would then attempt to have a conversation in broken English and Chinese. Eventually, we'd give up and I'd return my attention to the keyboard so that I could write.

These first few weeks living in Taiwan were confusing, but exciting. I had booked a room in the peaceful Mingsheng community of Taipei, filled with retirees and small food stands that opened at the whims of their owners. It was the perfect place. I was able to slow down and be with myself for what felt like the first time in my life. I deepened into this slowness, and as I did, I noticed the pressures from back home start to lose their power over me.

After writing, I would attempt to teach myself some basic Chinese from the textbook that Erv had loaned me. Eventually, I'd head out into the city to wander. Down the street an elderly couple ran a "Fàntuán," (飯糰 or rice ball) stand for a few hours in the morning and I'd go there to practice ordering in Chinese. It took me a couple of weeks to successfully understand the options, but the couple was thoroughly entertained by my curiosity and willingness to learn. By the second week, I had established myself as a regular, only having to say a simple hello, to which they'd reply, "Fàntuán? Jīdàn?" (飯糰? 雞蛋?) and I would nod to confirm my order.

Many days, I would walk and walk, trying to build up the courage to try out a phrase I had been practicing with Google Translate. I'd approach a food stand, but then chicken out at the last minute, sometimes delaying eating for hours. But there was something nice about this basic fear of making a fool of myself. I felt like a beginner, and more simply, I felt human. Back home, I always knew what I was doing. I had plans and was good at executing them. In Taiwan, I was often uncomfortable and didn't quite know what was happening around me. But it was a discomfort that made me curious. I wanted to see where it took me.

One day, I found myself in the expansive Da'an Forest Park. I meandered around the park taking pictures of trees I had never seen before and felt pulled to a cluster of bamboo tied together in a way that made it look like a giant green mushroom. I sat down on a park bench and read for a while. I felt my chest expand, filled with a deep-seated gratitude and sense of love for the world. I had the confusing feeling of being totally lost while also completely at home. It didn't make any sense: I had spent less than a month of my life in Taiwan and couldn't speak or read the language. But I felt more connected to myself than ever.

Part of this was the deep connection I felt while writing. As I wrote about my experiences in Taipei, my fear and excitement, and the work-related rabbit holes I was pulled into, I felt like one of the luckiest people in the world. The immediate joy I felt while writing and the spaciousness of my life was far better than anything I had ever experienced in the fourteen years I spent solidly pursuing the default path of success. I was writing at a kitchen table halfway across the world, for fun. It was so simple, but it felt so good. In these weeks, I started to understand the secret behind the phrase "find your passion and never work a day in your life." Previously I had always thought of a passion as something contained in a "dream job," but now I realized it could be a simple activity like writing. It was all I wanted to do in those weeks and only once I stripped my life down to the bare minimum could I actually notice my connection to this kind of work.

I was letting go of the deep-seated ideas that had shaped my life for so long, and I felt everything being turned upside down. This wasn't limited to my understanding of work; it extended to all aspects of my life. For years, the idea that I would travel *after* I found someone I wanted to marry had kept me from exploring the world. But the summer before I returned to Taiwan, I let go of the idea that I might find anyone at all. When I say let go, I mean it. I was at peace with possibly being on my own for the rest of my life. It's funny to look back, however, and realize that at that moment, I was only a couple of months away from meeting someone who would change my life.

One day, about a month after returning to Taiwan, I was feeling under the weather and sitting around scrolling my phone when Angie popped into my head. We had matched on a dating app during my initial trip to Taiwan months earlier but had failed to meet up. I sent her a message and she quickly replied. I was excited. We chatted for a bit and I asked if she wanted to go on a date. I had not prioritized dating in months, but something drew me to her. I pulled up her dating profile and noticed her mention of *The Art of Learning* by Josh Waitzkin. At worst, we would have a fun conversation about interesting books.

Two days later, we met at an intersection by a 7-11. As she waited for the crossing signal, I smiled at her standing there in her red top. I crossed the street and joined her. We immediately started walking toward the Buddha Tea House, a couple of blocks away, one of her favorite places in Taipei. Despite some awkward initial interactions, as we sat down, I was pulled into the conversation. She seemed to be coming alive in her own way and said she was starting to question many of the scripts she grew up with too. Even though she thought I would be, in her words, a "douchey, successful McKinsey guy," she eventually realized I was different from other people she had dated, and we connected over our interest in books, travel, family, and deciding to blow up our lives.

In my twenties, I had bought into the idea that women only like men with a promising career trajectory. This was true for some women, but my real error was assuming I would actually want to be with someone who valued me for my LinkedIn credentials. After I quit my job, I was surprised to find that I attracted different kinds of people, including women, who saw my lack of a plan and embrace of the unknown as a positive quality. While Angie later told me that she was a bit shocked at how I was spending my time in my first few weeks in Taiwan, wandering around listening to podcasts and reading in the park, she was also intrigued. *"Could someone really live like that?"* she asked herself. She had been going through her own career crisis, feeling trapped in her office job, but was starting to plot her own escape, and here I was a few steps ahead of her. We found comfort in each other's journeys, along with permission to share our boldest dreams.

After a year and a half of feeling lost after quitting my job, I started to feel like I was moving forward with my life. I wasn't following any specific path, but that no longer seemed important. I had found a connection to myself through writing, and with my awareness of that shift, I craved a new vision for life centered around aliveness. In meeting Angie, I had found someone who saw this way of living as obvious and it made me feel so much more confident. In conversations about our frustrations with the world, what we sought from life, and what really mattered, I started to feel at home. I was no longer alone. She shared my belief that there could be more to life than following the conventional, safe path and that there was definitely more to life than work.

In those first couple of months in Taiwan, everything shifted. I *knew* a different future was possible and I was ready to move toward it, no matter what.

2

FOLLOW YOUR ENERGY

I looked across the café and smiled as I made eye contact with Angie. We were just outside the central area of Chiang Mai in Thailand on a trip that had been her idea, a way to celebrate quitting her job at a technology think tank to start a new path in the fitness world.

I was on a video call talking to a potential client about taking on my first consulting project in nine months. It stirred up a mixture of emotions. Staring at the laptop, listening to the details of the project, I felt my body contract, my mind transported back to the free-lance work I had stopped doing earlier that year. At the same time, I knew I should be grateful. It was a remote project, one I could do while continuing to live abroad. I had not tried to find any work during the past few months, but I knew I could only avoid it for so long. After spending the day exploring temples and eating Thai food with Angie, this 30 minute call was hardly an inconvenience. In fact, this kind of work was a pragmatic way to extend an adventure I didn't want to end.

Since the moment we met, Angie and I had been inseparable. We explored Taipei night and day, and in our first month of dating, she had decided to leave her job too. In her final weeks, I often I received 9am calls proposing some adventure: "I'm not going to work today, want to go hiking?" These calls cracked me up. As someone who had been quietly rejecting work over the previous year, I was happy to have a co-conspirator in my search for a life not centered around work. We gave each other infinite permission to ignore the supposed responsibilities of adulthood. Having been single for so many years, and now finding myself in a situation that felt so perfect, I was happy to follow this relationship wherever it took me. A month after we started dating, Angie told me she was going to travel to Thailand for a month, and I happily postponed my flight back to the U.S. so I could join her.

In Thailand, we deepened our relationship on scooter rides through the mountains in Pai, disconnected from the world at a floating house on a remote lake, and contemplated life over tea and khao soi. The slowness and depth of everything we experienced were in stark contrast to my past attempts at dating in the U.S., where dates have to be scheduled around busy work lives. Angie and I joked that in just a few months, we had already spent more time together than career-focused couples do in a whole year. This felt important: she took quality time seriously and was willing to sacrifice things like money in return for connection, adventure, and love.

In those first months of our relationship, time seemed to stand still. We were lost in the present, two love drunk fools intoxicated by each other's presence. Until arriving in Thailand, neither of us dared to bring up the question of what would happen once I returned to the U.S. for Christmas. But during a short trip to the small town of Pai outside of Chiang Mai, I told her I wanted to come back to Taiwan and live there with her while she started her new job as a personal trainer. This was the first longer-term plan I had developed in over a year. It also marked the end of my blissful ignorance of life's realities during the previous three months of wandering through Taiwan and Thailand, not looking for paid work, and happily throwing myself fully into a new relationship. It was time to get serious, or at least serious enough to keep this journey alive.

Sitting on that video call with a potential client, I knew this meant I would have a hard time saying "no." The client, a friend, even joked that "Now that you have a girlfriend, you need to get serious about work!" They needed someone who could handle research and churn out high-quality PowerPoints with minimal supervision, which I could do in my sleep. When the call ended, I turned to Angie and explained why it was smart to take the project: "$7,500 will cover my cost of living for six months. I don't think it will be too much work. It's a good opportunity."

Because Angie was dealing with her own financial insecurity, having spent the last of her savings to take this trip to Thailand and then travel on to Hawaii, she was in no position to tell me not to worry about money. And even though it would have been a clear "no" if I had gone through Derek Sivers' decision prompt of "hell yeah or no" (which I later adopted), I didn't have the guts to turn the gig down.[1] The truth was, I still had financial worries, and while I had only been spending time on writing and creative work, I was still scared to fully build my life around those activities. The project money offered a temporary feeling of safety. *"Once this project is done, then I can really commit to the creative work,"* I told myself. I signed the contract that week.

Before returning to Taiwan to re-join Angie, I took a six-week detour to Bali in Indonesia. I was following another friend, Jonny Miller, who I had met at a conference the previous summer. We had hit it off instantly, connecting over our shared uncertainty, burnout experiences, and interest in building a life beyond the default path. The day after we met, he walked up to me and said, "Here, this is for you." It was a book by David Whyte, *The Three Marriages*. He said, "You have to read this." This is the book where I stumbled upon the phrase "The Pathless Path," which I instantly adopted to make sense of my journey and which ultimately resulted in my first book.

Jonny inspired me. I saw him as someone years ahead of me on a strange path, as he had lived all over the world and been on countless adventures. But the best thing about spending time with him was that he had a similar trust in the future. He was one of the first people I met who seemed to fully embrace the uncertainty of the world. During the conference, we had many conversations, and with him, I felt like I could be delusionally optimistic without having to prove I was on to anything.

When he emailed me a couple months after we met, I was already in Taiwan, but I had not yet met Angie. He was trying to rally a number of people to join him in Canggu, a small village in Bali, for a "creative residency." Reading the email, I felt an instant, full-body "Yes!" *Let's do this.* After meeting him and receiving his gift of the David Whyte book, I decided that I would prioritize spending time with people like him in the coming year, no matter where that took me. I was confident about the direction I was headed in, but still felt intimidated to be myself with most people in my life. I needed to find others that didn't need an explanation about where I was headed. Excited, I responded that my goals were to "learn something new, make one great, lifelong friend, and figure out where the pathless path takes me next." Which is wild, because not only did Jonny and I become closer, but Bali was where I started to commit, in my heart, to building a life around the work that mattered to me.

In Bali, I also started working on the client's project. I helped coordinate and lead customer interviews with people from the U.S. and Australia, which meant that I had to jump on calls as early as 4am. I dreaded those calls and would be plagued by sleep anxiety the night before. During the day, I would sit in the Tropical Nomad coworking space, intending to finish one or two hours of work in the morning. But without fail, I would procrastinate. I pulled up the PowerPoint slides that needed updating, and then did anything but work on them. I'd surf the web, join conversations around me, and sometimes leave altogether, taking a ride on my scooter without a destination. Even though the project did not require that many hours of actual work per week, I was filled with a slothful disinterest. My memory snapped back to the freelance project that I struggled with in the coworking office in Boston, and then to the final year in my full-time consulting job, when I often sat around all day, waiting until 5pm to power through the one hour of work I had to complete.

Over the next month in Bali, this project was like a cloud hanging over everything I did. It stifled my energy, and I became impatient with myself. I realized that I couldn't keep going like this indefinitely. My motivation to do this kind of work was running out. I didn't want to be a "taker" for projects like this anymore. Instead, I needed to trust the creative energy that had been taking over my life and be bolder about doubling down on the shift I had committed to in Taipei. Although my podcast and writing were starting to feel much more important, they still had to coexist with the consulting project. So I came up with a mantra for future decisions: "Coming alive over getting ahead." It was a reminder to choose work that lit me up, rather than work that merely serves to earn more money.

The truth was that for the previous year and a half I had been flailing rather than moving forward. I had "bought" time for myself by lowering my cost of living, but here I was, trading that time for work I didn't want to do. This is a common phase for those who embark on new paths, and it can be difficult to balance the confusing feelings of excitement about an uncertain journey with the fear-driven impulse to make money *right now*! During this phase, I still told people, especially those in my family, that I was a freelance consultant. I was scared of the judgment I might get for sharing the truth. The reality, however, was that my ability to function within my primary work identity as a "consultant" or even a "freelance consultant" had been extinguished.

At the end of that consulting project, I felt like I was in the tenth round of a boxing match, hoping the referee would end it for me. This is why freelancing is often a useful, but temporary, first stop for people on unconventional paths. It involves work you are good at and perhaps even enjoy somewhat, but if you try to turn this work into a business or your new identity, you end up creating a job for yourself that includes everything you wanted to escape in the first place.

The small village of Canggu in Bali was the perfect place to experience this confusing situation, as I was surrounded by many others trying to reinvent them-selves too. When I wasn't working on the client's project, I attended events at Outpost and Dojo coworking cafés and grabbed lunch with new friends at Café Vida and Shady Shack. I met a wide range of people: remote work-ers, entrepreneurs, digital nomads, and others just trying to escape some situation back home. There were people young and old and from many countries, but noticeably few Americans. I met people who worked in bars in Australia for a few months in between month-long surf sessions and local Indonesians who rejected the default path in Jakarta. And, of course, there were crypto people too, and I probably should have listened to them and bought a little more bitcoin. Overall, I loved the weird-ness and the energy of the place. It was perfect for that moment in my life.

With this backdrop, I was determined to push even harder into the unknown. I chose to let go of my free-lance consultant identity and see myself as a writer and creator optimizing my life around making those activi-ties possible. Which was scary. It meant sacrificing opportunities and the respect of others, but it felt right. The consulting project had pushed me to question my initial strategy: *Was I really just trying to live cheaply and work as little as possible? Or did I actually want something more?*

Luckily, I didn't have to work on the client's project most days, and in the six weeks I spent in Canggu, I threw myself into the work I cared about. Most mornings, I woke up energized, welcomed by the warm air, the cultural spirit, and the encouragement of many pathless wanderers. One of Jonny's friends, Jay Dike, even motivated me to double down on refining a consulting skills course that I had created months earlier, which I had not yet actively promoted. I had genuinely enjoyed building the course, originally as a way to share what I had learned in consulting with friends. Jay convinced me that there was a market for something like this, and plus, he saw that I needed a better way to make money than the project I kept complaining about.

During several meals at Ithaka Warung, overlooking the beach, he inspired me to take the course more seriously. With his help, I rebranded the course from *Strategy Toolkit* to *Think Like A Strategy Consultant*, moved the writing and videos from my personal site to a new platform I called *StrategyU*, and learned about digital marketing for the first time. Two months later, that course started generating income, and over the next few years, I slowly tinkered with it, building it into a source of modest income that funded most of my writing and creative explorations.

I would later call this "good enough" work. It didn't drain my energy like the consulting project, and it enabled me to do things I enjoy, like strategizing, writing, and even editing videos. It was also a pragmatic way to "buy" time to focus on the good work that I was going to do, no matter what. In the coming months, I mentally reclassified the team-based consulting projects that I had depended on early in my self-employment journey into the "break glass in case of emergency" category.

In Bali, people were incredibly open to sharing ideas and supporting each other. It was intensely optimistic. Everyone seemed eager to find ways to contribute. Inspired, I joined in the fun too, posting an offer on the local Facebook group to help people launch a podcast. I called it my "one hour podcast launch challenge." I wanted to help people cut the friction involved in putting their creative work into the world too, and experience the joy I had found from such work. Two people took me up on the offer, and while only one of those people is still running their podcast, it was so much fun. I even convinced Jonny to start taking action on launching his *Curious Humans* podcast. He shared a draft episode he recorded with David Whyte earlier that year and I couldn't contain my excitement. "Jonny, this is incredible. We need to get this into the world!"

It's clear to me now that by rooting for others, I was trying to revive my own inner confidence. The energy of Bali was intoxicating and it made me realize how receptive and responsive I was to the people around me. I loved this camaraderie of being surrounded by people on similarly uncertain, if not crazy, paths. It was such a contrast from my former work environments. Back then, aiming at the same goals as everyone else, it was impossible to avoid feeling like I was in a never-ending competition. All accomplishments came at someone else's expense. The corporate world fuels this non-zero-sum anxiety: if others are working late in the office, you convince yourself to stay late too. When others get promoted "ahead" of you, you feel insecure and envious because you think it means you aren't good enough. But when you find a path that is uniquely yours and you are able to fully inhabit it, you have no competitors. This is because the benefits of your unique path, like aliveness and connection to a certain kind of work, are not scarce resources. In Bali, I met people who were starting to understand this and I felt nothing but appreciation for them. I went out of my way to tell them, while reminding myself, too: "*Keep going, it matters.*"

Wrapping up the final week in Bali, I rode my scooter down the street to my favorite spot for smoothies. I felt more excited than I had in a long time. After six months of exploring Taiwan, Thailand, and Indonesia, and nearly two years of self-employment, I was starting to see that my real journey had never been about escaping work; instead, it was about searching for a deeper kind of work that I could commit to.

Once I stopped trying to be successful in other people's eyes, I was able to slow down, pay attention, and notice the things I did naturally, like writing. But this was not easy. It felt like I was turning a cruise ship in a new direction after following the same course for many years. Releasing my grip on the world was terrifying, but by letting go, I opened myself to a path that has helped me be more connected with myself than I ever thought possible.

People think that the moment you quit your job, your new path begins. But for me, it wasn't immediate. My new path only began as I was eating Mie Goreng and drinking a mango smoothie, sitting on a bean bag chair overlooking the sunset on Batu Balong beach.

As I sat there, I smiled, feeling tears of joy welling up inside of me, knowing that I was finally headed in the right direction.

3
COMMIT TO THE JOURNEY

In the seven years since I quit my consulting job, I've been called many things: lazy, unemployed, unambitious, a freeloader, ungrateful, reckless, stubborn, stupid, naive, and dumb. While I brushed these comments off at first, they stung a lot more after I moved abroad. I had embraced a life without a clear path or steady income. This made it difficult to justify my choices – not only to others but even to myself. When people criticized or questioned me, it amplified the uncertainty and fear I was already feeling and made me defensive. *"Don't you think it's selfish to be doing this?"* *"Aren't you wasting your career?"* I was already being hard enough on myself, I didn't need help from others.

I dealt with this discomfort by pulling away from the world, deepening into a season of solitude in Asia. Before moving abroad, I was caught in between two worlds. I felt pulled to the unknown, but was still physically in a place that had shaped every part of my life. Even after quitting my job and having far more freedom, I felt out of sync with the culture and energy of the U.S.. My move to Taiwan wasn't just about physical distance from home; it was also an attempt to find more mental and emotional space. I needed time to think, reflect, and process what was unfolding in my life.

In Taiwan, and then Thailand and Bali, I was able to ease into what I now realize was the first true "break" of my adult life. This period of spaciousness allowed me to drop into a natural phase of being lost, one that had been calling me for more than a year. It was in this space that great things started to emerge, like writing and my relationship with Angie. But it was also in this space that I started to viscerally feel the effects of my life choices. *Shit, what had I done? Did I really want ALL of this?*

In *The Way Home*, Ben Katt reflects on embracing a season of wandering during his own journey, writing, "after you leave home, the old maps — reliable and helpful for so long — no longer work."[1] In Taiwan, I was happily abandoning my old maps and scripts that told me what I *should* be doing, but was still relatively unprepared for what it might actually feel like. In those first months, I felt a whirlwind of emotions, from excitement to contentment to intense shame and failure. While I was determined to keep going, I couldn't hide from feeling like I was torching everything good in my life – the support of family, friends, and a vibrant career back home. Amidst these feelings, I didn't run from them. I turned inward, confronting deeper questions:

Who was I?

What did I want?

What would that mean for my life?

These questions, which I had long avoided, demanded my attention. For the first time, I embraced not knowing, understanding that uncertainty was now a permanent passenger on my path. I also realized that I might *never* be able to stop asking these fundamental questions. I surrendered to the nature of this new path I had chosen. At first, it was dizzying. But the more time I spent in this liminal state, the more comfortable I felt. I didn't mind the constant uncertainty, and I slowly started to realize that I wanted all of it: the good, bad and everything in between. I knew that the journey would be hard, but I was ready to accept everything in front of me.

This experience abroad was, in essence, an unplanned sabbatical. It was a prototype of a life I was headed toward at full speed while also a chance to slow down before moving forward. Before going abroad, it was impossible to commit to this new path. I didn't have enough time and space to be with myself and notice that a new Paul had been emerging over the past several years, even before I quit my job. This break, the first of more than two weeks in my adult life, brought clarity. I recognized the creative, hyper-curious, and bold person actively steering my life in a new direction. Despite my fears, I didn't need to pretend or please others. I could fully own my dreams.

The transformative power of sabbaticals remains underrated. While they are gaining popularity, many people still feel tremendous guilt about taking a break from work without a plan. It's just not something most people do. It's normal to save for years for a dream home or for university education for your kids, but when people think about saving or planning for a sabbatical in the same way, they dismiss the possibility. But a sabbatical doesn't need to be a major sacrifice. If you consider a sabbatical a three-month break in the 500 or more months that most adults spend working from ages 22 to 65, it represents less than one percent of an average working life. A small price to pay to discover something that might radically improve your life.

When people do take a conscious break from work, many wish they had done it sooner. Not working forces you to be with yourself and is a way to fast track going after the life you want. But arriving at this point does not come naturally. In the first few weeks, and sometimes months, of sabbaticals, most people awaken to work scripts that had been running in the background of their lives. As they begin to move away from these scripts, a tension emerges. For me, I had to face the fact that I walked away from a path that everyone around me saw as the ultimate prize. Others struggle with feelings of not being productive: when they don't have a "workday" to show up for, they must reckon with questions like, "*Who am I without work?*" and "*Am I allowed to simply be with myself?*"

Caitlyn Lubas, who decided to take a year-long sabbatical after she was laid off from her Product Manager job, reflected on this tension: "It's been four months since I've stopped working, and it's taken me about this long to become at peace with doing nothing and being 'unproductive' when my body and mind crave rest."[2] In my experience, this phase of "doing nothing" is essential. For me, it is how I started to pay attention and get to know myself again. I was able to fully reawaken the effortless curiosity and energy of my younger self. Others report that they rediscover forgotten hobbies, kickstart creative projects, and start to dream in new directions about the future.

In an essay detailing a one-year sabbatical from her job, my friend Cécile Marion wrote about a wide range of emergent interests, including writing, studying neuroscience, learning design and website design, reading classic books, creating visual summaries of books and podcasts, and more. As she concluded: "All this made me realize just how many opportunities for meaningful work would come up if I simply followed my curiosity, created things as I explored, and shared some of those with the world."[3]

By taking a break and learning to follow their interests, people start to ask new questions, ones that plant the seeds for a much bigger vision of life. It is this vision that lets them keep searching for good work, even as they start to feel the pressure to "get serious." As Cécile said, "I used to be scared to lose my job. I was worried I would not find anything else. I am not worried anymore. This experience has helped me shift from a scarcity mindset to an abundance mindset." Cécile returned to work for an entire year before deciding to walk away again, this time with more determination to build a life around good work. The search can be a frustratingly long journey, but for many, including me, it is one that feels impossible to abandon.

The journey of finding and committing to good work is filled with twists, turns, and moments of doubt. By creating space in our lives, we not only let good things blossom, but also embrace the discomfort that we spent so long running away from. We start to see our paths more clearly and realize that we had been doing things against our nature. In a reflection after a year of taking a sabbatical from her Physician Assistant job, Samantha Varghese wrote, "When I think about how I was willing to work a 'higher level' job for money I don't need just so other people would not judge me, I see how I was living in a delusion where the trivial was disguised as important."[4]

This clarity can be powerful but it can also be unsettling. It forces you to lean away from life paths that will be seen as successful. Luckily, Samantha has been on sabbatical at the same time as her sister, Michelle, who took a break from the tech industry. They've been able to make sense of it together. As Samantha says, "This journey isn't about never working again; it's about working in a way that honors who we have become. So, while Michelle and I may still engage in work, we will not be stepping into the same river because we have changed, and so has the world around us." This is exactly what good work is about: noticing the season of life you are in, right now, and seeing what work you are called to do.

In contrast to a conventional life built around constant work, career progress, and financial outcomes, searching for good work requires slowness, experimentation, and introspection. Despite the abundance of formulas and playbooks promising easy answers for monetizing your passion, building an audience, or becoming a 7-figure entrepreneur, committing to this path is hard. It's comforting to believe that you can simply spin up a side gig and replace your salary before quitting your job. Or that building a business is as easy as picking the right niche. Or that a perfect morning routine and productivity stack is the key to unlocking your dream life. Unfortunately, what works for someone else will rarely work the same for you. It would be convenient if well-structured self-help books translated into foolproof paths we could follow, but reality remains far more complex.

This is why when people ask me, "How can I do what you're doing?" I can't tell them what they want to hear. They want easy answers, a shortcut to a future state of success. But the path that will lead us to the life we want is uniquely our own, inevitably filled with the exact challenges we'd rather avoid.

Most people have an acute sense of the challenges that lay ahead. They can predict the criticism they'll face and the insecurity they'll feel. This is why many, including me, refuse the "call to adventure" as long as possible. Before quitting my job, I spent several years critiquing the corporate world from within, convinced I could help "fix" it. But really, this was an elaborate way of deflecting blame onto the "system" rather than taking responsibility for my own life. Simply, I was terrified to admit that I did not fit into this world I had worked so hard to enter, and I was scared to find my own way out.

Like many others, I had been in steady motion since childhood, going from kindergarten to middle school to high school to university to senior manager. This convinced me that everything we seek in life can be obtained by following a similar clear path. But searching for good work is not about finding a perfect job or a path that others understand. It's about developing a sense of connection to yourself and your work and learning to trust a vague sense of knowing that comes from deep inside of you. Softening into this process takes time. I first experienced this in Taipei, where I had enough space in my life to slow down and pay attention, committing to the journey of good work.

So the only reasonable answer I can give to the question of "How can I do what you are doing?" is this: fully commit to the journey, challenges and all. Once you do, don't give up. Keep going. Take the search for good work seriously.

And I'd be a little more skeptical about this, except for the fact that I've had a front row seat to my wife Angie's search for good work too.*

---

* Yes, we got married, about a year after we met in Taiwan. Wasn't it obvious it was headed in that direction?

4

HAVE FAITH IN GOOD WORK

Angie had spent her twenties chasing the life she thought she wanted: attending a top graduate school in the U.S., followed by a good job in the technology industry in Taiwan. But as she turned 30, she had the same impulse I had years earlier, to run away from it all.

Our relationship started in the wake of this shift and I was able to have a front row seat to the start of her search for good work. It was a relief to see, quite clearly, that she experienced many of the same ups and downs that I did years earlier. Finally, someone else could understand what I was going through. At the same time, it was painful to watch her struggle and I wanted to help. But despite my deep understanding of unconventional paths and the complexities of people's relationships with work, I was unable to accelerate her journey in any meaningful way. It helped me realize that searching for and finding good work is a personal journey, one that everyone must go through in their own way.

After she quit her job in tech shortly after we started dating, she started a new path as a fitness trainer. Within only a few months, she came to the painful realization that she loved *learning* about fitness but didn't enjoy being a coach as a job. It sucked the joy out of it. She decided to make the best of the situation by creating opportunities to do related work. She convinced the owner of the gym to let her launch an interview show for their YouTube channel and wrote articles for their website, but she still felt unsatisfied. After almost a year at the gym, she felt stuck once again. She was hard on herself, ashamed that just a year earlier she had told everyone in her life that this was her "dream job."

Toward the end of that year, she decided to participate in an online course I was running, an early prototype of the ideas that ended up in *The Pathless Path*. During one of the weeks, we had an "action challenge," where people had to put something out into the world in under a week. I suggested she might try launching her own podcast because of how much she loved learning about fitness. She accepted the challenge, and launched her podcast *Curious Barbell* soon after.

Around this time, she decided she would leave the gym. It was clear that personal training was not her good work. Nevertheless, she still had hope that she could build a business in the fitness world. Her podcast was one of the first of its kind to launch in Taiwan, and she quickly built a sizable audience of passionate listeners. She created an online fitness course for beginners with a friend and launched a fitness community for the Taiwanese diaspora. Everything she started seemed to "work" in terms of finding an audience and gaining interest, and she clung to these projects as we left Taiwan to live nomadically.

I loved seeing her succeed with these projects, but over time, her own interest faded. She realized she was doing it for her own personal learning journey, and never felt comfortable running a business or being a public "creator" in the fitness industry. The work shifted from something she enjoyed to tasks that became painful to complete. I would watch her work late into the night, complaining about it, and I would say, "You realize you work for yourself and you don't have to keep doing this, right?"

But she felt like she did. After we left Taiwan, I was the sole income-earner and she felt pressure to contribute, wanting to feel, in her words, "like she was my equal." On top of this, she had already left personal training behind, so quitting this emerging "creator" path, which had clear signs of opportunity, seemed foolish and would be admitting defeat, again. I hated seeing her go through all of this. When I tried to encourage and support her, it often amplified her insecurities. "I may be having some success, but I'm still not making any money," she would tell me. But I never cared about that. I had risked everything to find work that mattered to me, and I wanted her to be able to do the same.

Two years after initially leaving Taiwan, we moved back to the U.S. and she continued to search for work that would earn more money. One of her ideas was to join a tech company. Now that she could legally work in the U.S., she considered finding an impressive high-paying job. I connected her with friends and classmates in the tech industry and helped her practice interviews. But deep down, I sensed that this was just another distraction. She never seemed that excited about it. I could see that her path to good work likely involved something creative. I just had no idea how long it would take for her to believe it too.

For the next year, she kept experimenting. She explored art, freelanced for internet creators, kept applying for jobs, wrote, and did many other things. Nothing clicked. After becoming pregnant, Angie started to let go of the idea of finding a job in the corporate world, but still felt the pressure to reliably make money. She had internalized the idea that to be a successful mother, she also needed to be a successful worker. She started doing more freelancing projects and found that she was good at it, but all I noticed was the tremendous amount of energy it took her just to start working and how depleted she was after finishing the work. At the end of one project, the client was incredibly happy with her contributions and offered her a part-time position.

She told him she would consider the offer after giving birth.

For the first few months after Michelle was born, we both were fully present, drunk with the joy of being new parents. But as I returned to some of my work a few months later, Angie started to pressure herself to figure out her next step. She asked herself, *"Should I join the client's team?"* As she contemplated this idea and we explored what it might mean for our family, I grew incredibly frustrated. We had decided to fully co-parent in the first year, and not rely on daycare, so anything we worked on would involve trade-offs. I knew that this project might make her feel better, but I sensed it was no more than that.

I had given her immense space and support for years, but this time, I felt I had to challenge her. I said, "Look, you are an incredible mother and I just don't think it's worth it for you to spend less time with Michelle to do this project. I'm happy to support you fully if you choose this path, but you obviously don't really care about it. Isn't that what we're trying to do, build our family around doing things we really care about?"

Angie was frustrated, feeling hopeless, and yelled, "If I don't take this project, what am I supposed to do? I don't want to just be a full-time mom!"

"Why not write a book?" I said.

"No way! Just because you've had success with your book doesn't mean everyone should write a book!" she yelled back.

I sighed, frustrated, wishing she would see herself in a more positive light.

I made my case: "Angie! How can you not see who you really are? After all these years? Every time you share your writing with the world, you get these crazy reactions. Even when you had no audience, you'd share these random posts on Facebook or in a newsletter and every time you get these long, thoughtful responses. I get those sometimes, but nothing like yours. You're good at it and channeling something powerful. Why are you so scared to follow that?"

As I had said this, she had been withdrawing from the conversation, drifting into the other room. Standing in the hallway, she countered, "I don't have traditional success or followers like you. No one will want to read my story. I won't make money like you did."

This was the same thing she always said. She was a master at dismissing anything positive I had to say about her.

I responded, trying to make my case while also trying to get her to understand how hard my journey had been too: "It doesn't matter. I didn't write a book for the money. I wrote it because it was hard and it was a way to do something that mattered to me. You always claim you want to find something to commit to, but you always give up. A book is a long journey. Maybe writing a book will help you finally understand how to commit to something."

In her own book, Angie recounted what happened next:[*]

> *The idea of doing something for the sake of practicing commitment shook me. He was right. Over the past few years, whether it was running a podcast, creating courses, or freelancing, impostor syndrome always led me to self-destruct whenever I saw any potential for success. Although I ignored his suggestion for several months, the idea of writing a book slowly took root in my mind.*
>
> *I decided to test writing what I called a "mini-memoir" in a short writing challenge hosted by the Write of Passage community. After sharing my first essay, someone asked a question which made me question my perspective on life. It shocked me. I had thought one thing about my relationship with my mother, and the question made me look at it in a completely new way. It was intense and I decided to stop writing for a while to process what happened. However, when I stopped, I felt pulled back to writing. At that moment, I also understood that perhaps my claim that writing is painful wasn't because I*

---

[*] Angie's deep in the 3rd draft of her book. It's going to be great. Follow along here for updates: angiecreates.io

hated writing, but because deep down, I knew that writing had the power to change my life.

I completely abandoned the project until we returned to Taiwan, visiting my family with our daughter. Upon arriving, I started updating my stories about growing up in Taiwan. I started writing again, committing to a book but doing it as a fictional narrative. I wrote that version for weeks before realizing I couldn't hide. I had to write the real story.

Once I made the shift, I started taking it seriously and through writing, was able to drop into a state of flow I had never experienced before. It was a feeling of pure self-belief and surrender. I finally understood what Paul meant about not worrying about selling his book and enjoying the process. I didn't know if I would sell a single book but it no longer mattered. Despite my mind still generating a million reasons to quit, I slowly started to let a deeper trust in life guide me. I knew that my only task was to write with focus, intensity, and sometimes, a bit of madness. The rest, I left to fate. I knew that no consulting project was going to help me see myself as a valuable person and mother. The book was my path. It was my good work.

Watching this transformation filled my heart with love and admiration. I would have given anything to help

Angie see herself in a more positive light. And through writing, she was finally experiencing it.

What was shocking to me was that this shift happened in Taiwan, where our schedule was less than ideal. In the first month we shuffled between three different apartments before settling in one place for two months. We traveled back and forth to visit her parents in Taichung every other week and filled our schedule with many overnight trips around the island, taking advantage of our daughter's ability to sleep anywhere, and excited to bring her to our favorite places.

But despite the hectic schedule, Angie continued writing. On a bus ride to visit some friends across town, halfway through our trip, she pulled out her laptop on a crowded bus in Taipei.

"What are you doing?" I asked.

"I'm writing," she said.

I looked around and laughed. It was crazy. The bus whipped around the corner of a busy intersection, and she was locked in, with her laptop propped up on the diaper bag on her lap. I scanned the bus, seeing people standing shoulder to shoulder beside us and Michelle parked in the stroller right in front of us. I looked at Angie excitedly and proclaimed, "This is it, this is it!" She smirked and kept typing.

For more than five years I had been trying to convince her that writing could potentially be her thing. But she always had a reason why it wasn't possible. She was convinced that she needed to find the right job or freelance or make money some other way. But now here she was, without resistance, pulling out a laptop in the most absurd location to do her good work, to release her thoughts onto the page.

Watching her go through this lengthy process was painful. I would have done anything to help her avoid some of the challenges she faced. But everyone must follow their own path. Fortunately, and most importantly, she never gave up. Perhaps her delusionally optimistic husband played a role, but really, she has the same impulse that I do: she needs to do things that matter to her to feel alive. Here she reflects on her current relationship with writing almost a year after this shift:

I'm almost a year into the writing process for this book. It has changed my life. Through writing, I am transported into a state of awe and wonder. I now understand that the answers that open me up to life might not be found by exploring the world, visiting various countries, but within myself. In the last couple of months, that same client tried to recruit me to join their team once again. This time, I refused without a second thought, because I knew that more important than curing my insecurities with a high-paying job, I had something much more significant to accomplish.

Remarkably, Angie was able to find her good work even after becoming a mother and taking on far more responsibility. Some say that for parents, this journey is impossible, but in our experience, Angie and I have both found a tremendous sense of clarity about our work *after* having children. The responsibility creates real constraints and an urgency to eliminate work that doesn't matter. Plus, we want to inspire Michelle to dream big and to unleash her creativity into the world too.

As I write this, Angie is taking care of our daughter. Tomorrow we'll swap, and she'll write while I'm in "dad mode." Watching her move forward with her book project inspires me and injects more energy into this book too. Through writing, she has also found a lens to understand my sometimes maniacal commitment to my path and work. Before, she could never really figure out how I kept writing for so many years without any external success or the encouragement of a large audience. She would always link my success to my consulting experience. "It's easy for you, you worked at the best companies," she would say, and "You are the wonder boy." This always made me wish we could travel back in time together so I could show her how I had also struggled for years and that my current path resulted from a slow and confusing journey of false starts. But now that she's moving ahead on her own journey, she gets it. My current accomplishments don't make me some special superhuman, it's just that I'm a little further along on my path. This realization has injected our relationship and family with meaning and gives us more confidence that we can build a life around doing what matters to us and support our daughter to do the same.

Once you've experienced the joy of good work, *not* experiencing this state makes you take cultivating and protecting good work even more seriously. I was 33 years old, without any paid work, far from home in an apartment in Taipei when I realized that writing might be my good work. But I had already spent nearly fifteen years doing on-and-off-again experiments searching for something I didn't quite understand during a chaotic career of job changes and increasing dissatisfaction. It was striking how long it had taken me to realize my interest in writing even after it had started to occupy most of my time. Those moments of joy I found in writing, even when I didn't see it as "work," were always clues trying to point me in the right direction. It was always right in front of me.

The most important thing is that I never gave up. When I slowed down enough to pay attention, I found my good work. And once I found it, everything in my life shifted. My life became filled with a certain kind of magic, which injected me with a sense of possibility and trust that everything would work out. Good work has been a steady "home" I can return to throughout this entire process. It has transformed my entire relationship to life itself and the contrast between my previous path and my current one is stark. It's not simply a change in the kind of work I do, it's a fundamental shift in how I show up in the world. All I have to do now is stay connected to it.

I watched Angie go through many of the same challenges I faced years earlier. It was painful to see her struggle and not be able to help her more. But she never gave up, and as I've watched her soften into her true nature, I've been further convinced that finding a connection with good work can have a profound positive impact on one's life.

But to experience any of this, you must maintain faith that this is possible.

PART TWO
REWRITE YOUR WORK STORY

"Don't be a career. The enemy of most dreams and intuitions, and one of the most dangerous and stifling concepts ever invented by humans, is the 'Career.' A career is a concept for how one is supposed to progress through stages during the training for and practicing of your working life.

There are some big problems here. First and foremost is the notion that your work is different and separate from the rest of your life. If you are passionate about your life and your work, this can't be so. They will become more or less one. This is a much better way to live one's life."[1]

— STEVE JOBS

"Find a subject you care about and which you in your heart feel others should care about. It is this genuine caring, and not your games with language, which will be the most compelling and seductive element in your style."[2]

— KURT VONNEGUT

5
FIND A POSITIVE EDGE

I'm not sure when, but at some point in my childhood, I began thinking that I was not enough. To prove my worth, I needed to accomplish things. I needed to become somebody.

This idea seeped into my subconscious and I never questioned it. The real problem was that I fully embraced it during an extremely vulnerable period: adolescence. In high school, I was at the peak of my insecurity. In the classroom, I was confident. But beyond that, I never felt comfortable in my own skin. I had been one of the last in my class to hit puberty, and when I finally started to grow in my junior year, it was as if I had been stretched vertically. I was now six feet tall and had gone from one of the shortest people in my class to one of the tallest. But I had not gained any weight. I looked like a walking stick figure, and I was hyper-conscious of this fact. My friends even declared they would throw me a party when I finally weighed 100 pounds.

In my senior year, despite my insecurity, I built up the courage to ask someone to the prom. She said "Yes," but there was an additional approval needed: I had to ask her father's permission. I agreed to the unusual request, not feeling I had any choice. The following weekend, I went to their house. Upon arrival, I met the family in the kitchen before being summoned to the back room by her father. Walking into the small room, we sat down across from each other. As he settled into his chair, he pulled out some chewing tobacco and tucked it under his lip. Leaning back slightly, he seemed to be taking some joy my discomfort. I tried to mask my fear, likely to little effect.

We sat there for what felt like minutes. Finally, staring at me, he asked "What are your intentions with my daughter?"

I fumbled my way through the conversation. The disconnect between his CIA-level interrogation and the fact that I had literally just asked someone out for the first time in my life was jarring. If I had been confident enough to speak my true feelings, I would have said, "Sir, this whole situation is unnecessary. You don't have to scare me. I am already terrified. I have not gone on a single date in high school. I still look like a 13-year old. My confidence when it comes to women is non-existent."

We sat there for what felt like hours, talking about my plans for prom night and then for my future. Eventually, as I shared some of my achievements, like my class rank and the fact that I had an academic scholarship to college, he seemed to relax. Through the lens of extrinsic success, I could stand out. It was where I shined.

From that moment on, I relied on a formula: follow the successful path. Get good grades, and do what's seen as impressive. This became easier at university, where almost everyone around me was also trying to do the same. I felt great because I was "good" at school, or at least the "get the highest grades" part of it. As I racked up awards and honors, and kept my full scholarship, I won the admiration of others. In the years that followed, the identity of the achiever became a safe cocoon where I could hide from my insecurities while projecting outward confidence. I even found support for my fear of dating. When people praised me for "not wasting time on women," I felt validated. *They see me!*

This game, focusing on success in school and then the workplace, *did* increase my self-confidence, but I had created a trap for myself. My approach to life depended on playing a never-ending game. Subconsciously, I knew that if I stopped moving forward I would have to face my underlying insecurities. So I didn't stop. I kept going for more than a decade, always eyeing the next step.

Hustle bros love the phrase, "chips on shoulders put chips in pockets," as if feeling deficient is the best motivation to succeed in the world. Perhaps this approach can work for a time, as it did for me, and maybe it's even a necessary phase in life. But for most people, this way of orienting your life eventually demands a reckoning.

When I quit my job, many years later, I discovered that I had so deeply internalized the achiever identity that I struggled to turn off that part of my mind. It was as if I had a software program running on autopilot. When I felt uncertain about my financial position, my mind developed ten ways to make money. When I felt uncertain about what to do next, it generated a plan that others would approve. When I realized that this program could stay running for the rest of my life, I was determined to lessen its influence, no matter how painful. But this decision left me feeling immobilized. Without the autopilot voice to guide me, I had nothing to lean on and I felt increasingly lost in that first year of self-employment. I also realized that what I had really been doing for so many years was constructing an impressive fortress around my own inner world. By focusing on traditional metrics of success, I could look outward and into the future. This mindset, or really, a sort of trance, produced what many people call an "edge." But this edge was both a protector and a burden. It shielded me from uncertainty and my own fears, yet demanded constant maintenance via a steady stream of future plans and goals.

In the first year after I quit my job, when I stopped pursuing achievements, my edge began to erode and the fortress crumbled. I had no choice but to be present with many of the emotions I had suppressed and avoided. It was intense. I could fully feel the inadequacy of not feeling attractive to women when I was younger, the embarrassment of hundreds of rejections throughout my career, the frustration of never finding a job I liked, and the shame of throwing it all away without a plan, still dissatisfied and confused. But if I had waited longer to quit, it would just have been harder. I was grateful for the opportunity to face myself and grow up. I had been floating with the tide for too long, afraid of what I might feel if I swam in a different direction.*

When I moved to Taiwan and committed to writing, something unexpected happened: I stopped drinking. Without any effort at all, alcohol vanished from my life, and nearly six years later, I rarely think about it. At the time I didn't think much about it. I had been changing so much in my life and that was just one more thing that shifted. But looking back, it's clear that alcohol had been a vital part of maintaining my edge. Up until I quit my job, I drank most weekends, convinced it was never an issue because I knew "real" alcoholics that drank every day. I was sober every Monday through Thursday and then would let it rip on the weekend. I was a card-carrying member of the "Thank God It's Friday" club. I never stayed in on a single weekend in my twenties, always desperate to have plans. The truth? I was scared to be with myself.

---

* Friendly nod to Hunter S. Thompson's letter, "The ninth path," (Source:"Letters of Note" by Shaun Usher)

Alcohol helped me ignore the underlying discomfort in my life. I might be frustrated at work but I was always less than five days away from the next chance to party and run from those emotions. I didn't see it as a problem because I found so many willing co-conspirators. I told myself and others I was happy, but in reality I was just surrounded by others all numbing themselves too. If you stay in an anesthetized state long enough, you accept that this never ending cycle of low-grade anxiety and the need to escape is your destiny. When I started to go after the life I wanted and stopped hiding from myself, I had little use for alcohol and other coping mechanisms.

But this meant I had to face my fears. I couldn't hide. Despite this, I started to find wisdom in the scary emotions of life. I accepted that uncertainty is an unavoidable companion on a pathless path. As a result, I developed a capacity to make decisions not as a *reaction to* certain emotions, trying to make them go away, but instead to make decisions *together with* my emotions, understanding that they would always be with me on my journey.

I found such power in this reframe.

If fear is always a companion, it is futile to push it away. If uncertainty can never be solved, you have more freedom in terms of how you choose to spend your time and which risks you take. If insecurity is always present, wholeheartedly committing to the work that matters to you becomes much more sensible. And if doubt creeps in, you can welcome it: "Oh it's you, the doubt monster? Nice to see you again!" This shift in perspective emboldened me. *If the journey of good work means I might feel somewhat inadequate, so what?* As the poet Robert Frost wrote, "The best way out is through."[1]

When I moved to Taiwan, I was fully embracing all of these feelings and as I did that, I stopped needing to run from myself. But this process is hard and when people tell me they are scared of losing their edge, this is what they are really afraid of. They fear letting go of strategies, often enacted years ago, that help them feel safe, and that let them avoid facing what's underneath. They are uncomfortable not having a plan and having to slow down into the inherent uncertainty of the world. However, the search for good work means stepping directly into this discomfort. I tell people explicitly, "The journey might suck, but it might also be worth it." Unfortunately, you won't know until you are on the other side.

Letting go of a life strategy that seems to be working can be terrifying. For me, it meant stepping away from a formula for life that provided me with money, status, and real confidence. I loved feeling competent and being good at what I did. So realizing that I never wanted to return to that world initially filled me with grief. I *do* miss telling people about my impressive achievements and watching their eyes light up with instant respect. It was so simple and the lack of that kind of reaction is still clearly noticeable on my current path. Now, instead of igniting admiration, I often trigger people's deepest fears.

Mourning the loss of my inner achiever has been challenging. In the first year after leaving my consulting career behind, I craved support from the people around me. But I didn't know how to obtain it in this new mode of life. In the past, approval and support were automatic byproducts of my accomplishments. On my new path, I had nothing tangible that would "prove" I was doing something worthwhile. Plus, I felt completely responsible for my situation. I was the one who had chosen this path. *It was my fault that I was in this situation and I should not complain.* Eventually, I admitted to myself that I did desire appreciation and that it was okay to want this. Luckily, I've found many other people who are absorbed in creative work or have left traditional paths, and their encouragement provides a powerful source of confidence to keep going.

Life transitions are so tricky because while you are happy to consciously abandon *some* parts of yourself, you also unintentionally let go of other parts that meet important needs and desires. But what surprises many people, including me, is that by shedding a former identity, you often open yourself up to new ways of orienting your life that can be far more expansive than you ever thought possible.

My initial drive to achieve "success" was powerful enough to help me reach impressive goals. But it was also a weak form of motivation because it kept me doing things I didn't want to do in pursuit of goals I did not truly care about. If someone had challenged me to a fight over my job, after a moment of incredible confusion, I would have immediately said, "Take it." My heart was never in it.

On my current path, I am filled with an intense but grounded sense of zeal and would gladly fight someone to protect my time, freedom, and sense of wonder that I have on this path. *"Oh, you want this path? Fight me for it!!"* Luckily, no one wants to challenge me to a duel to acquire my life, but that doesn't make me cherish it any less. In Bali, my decision not to rely on consulting income was scary, but it also allowed me to fully embrace a new form of motivation that has since taken over my life.

A post by investor and generally curious human Patrick O'Shaughnessy perfectly captures his own shift from his initial path to one that feels more sustainable: "People think great accomplishment requires 'grit' and 'grinding,' and I have nothing against those things, and surely tons of the great outcomes were just made possible by extreme grinders... but, I never feel like I'm grinding when I do the thing I like doing." He realized that "the best long term fuel source is some repeated act that energizes you in a way that then lets you become a generative person." Once he stumbled onto this secret, everything opened up for him. But similar to me, he's found it challenging to explain this insight without relying on clichés like this: "If you just do what you love, incredible but unpredictable things will happen."[2]

Similar to O'Shaughnessy, leaning into this new way of being has led me to a life that feels full. I now feel drawn to a much bigger version of my life, one filled with depth and meaning that involves the full range of emotions from sadness to joy and from anger to wonder. I no longer want to go through the motions of life. I know what that feels like. I don't want to hide, I want to do it full out.

On your own unique path, you are on a slipstream of your own creation. You can move freely with agency and make decisions that make sense only to you. Early in my life, the desire to escape my insecurity was a powerful motivator and it was easy to take action: figure out what's impressive to others and aim for that. This approach "worked," but it resulted in a life that became increasingly fragile. When I quit my job and didn't want to go back, many people were surprised. *"How do you give it all up?"*

Easy. I found something worth fighting for.

On my current path, my only goal is to keep going. This is easy to commit to because I've experienced a radical shift in my day-to-day reality. Instead of pushing forward, driven by a sense of lack, I'm being pulled by a profound psychological richness that I experience from being in the flow of my own interests.

As I've embraced this new source of motivation, a "positive edge," my entire approach to life has shifted. I feel lighter and carry around far less anxiety about the future. While this path requires far more discipline, emotional awareness, and reflection, the payoff is worth it. By softening into my own nature and focusing on what really matters, I've discovered a powerful truth: the only true and worthwhile edge is deeply caring about what you do.

6

DON'T MISTAKE A GOOD JOB
FOR GOOD WORK

For the first 32 years of my life, I believed that everything we seek from life can be found by first landing a "good" job. By "good" job, I mean the kind that comes with an impressive paycheck, a clear path up the corporate ladder, and a business card with a Fortune 500 logo. This story wasn't just mine, it was everywhere around me. I saw it on television shows where the father dutifully headed to the office each morning. I overheard it in conversations among adults pointing out the importance of good benefits packages and health insurance coverage. I experienced it participating in the frenzied pursuit of the "best" companies during recruiting season on campus. The message I absorbed was clear: secure one of these coveted jobs and everything will be okay.

But our obsession with getting "good" jobs undermines our ability to notice the kinds of work that may not fill a bank account, but will nourish our souls. For far too long, this blind spot kept me from waking up to the reality that "good" jobs do not always contain good work. As I searched for a "dream job" in my twenties, my job-shaped assumptions limited the possibilities of my life.

Now I haven't had a "good" job in more than seven years and nothing about my current work resembles a conventional job. Most of my writing happens in the three-hour blocks I schedule each week, and my years are filled with seasonal flows of intense work and leisure. But the lines between work and non-work are fuzzy. Since I love thinking about ideas and exploring my curiosity, "work" is happening all the time in conversations with friends, on long bike rides, in the shower, and at the gym.

The introduction to my first book even came to me while taking a break from writing in the small beach town of Kenting in the south of Taiwan. While we had intended to travel the world for two years after leaving the country, we returned less than a year later, derailed by Covid-19 travel restrictions. Despite this, life was pretty good. We were spending extended time in several places around the island, the first time Angie had ever done this in her home country.

From the beautiful mountains and simplicity of life in Hualien to the intense green of the rice fields in Fuli, Taiwan offered endless inspiration. I cherished slow, meandering bike rides through the car-free National

Taiwan University campus on my way to Chinese class in Taipei, and now, I was embracing the excited beach town energy of Kenting. Throughout that year, my surroundings fueled my creativity, enabling me to be happily lost in the flow of writing.

Despite the progress I was making on the book, the introduction felt like an impossible puzzle. I kept trying to find the words to bring alive the essence of the book but kept coming up short. One morning, I found myself increasingly annoyed, staring at the document on my laptop. Angie noticed.

"Take a break," she suggested. "Go for a scooter ride. You've been at this for weeks."

After three years together, I knew not to ignore her advice. I walked out of the hotel room we had been staying in for the past few weeks in Kenting. I put on my helmet and rode out of the driveway onto the main road. As I drove, I took several deep breaths.I glanced over to the mountains and smiled. This was exactly the kind of life I wanted and realizing this, a feeling of gratitude washed over me.

As I thought back to the introduction I was struggling with, all I could think was, *Why is this part so hard?* As I continued to ride, I noticed a tightness in my chest. I took a few deep breaths. It started to dawn on me. It was fear. I was scared to share what I really thought. I was attempting to write a book, not another short essay. It would be read by anyone in the world, for the rest of my life. I had been writing about my alternative approach to work for years, but had always hedged my thoughts. Now, there was no hiding. More importantly, I wasn't just writing this book for others, I was writing it for myself. Upon realizing this, tears began to stream down my face. I pulled to the side of the road and continued crying. After a few deep breaths, I relaxed. I opened up my notes app and wrote in a stream of consciousness:

Helping people live courageously so that they can thrive is one of the most important things in the world. I want to see people live the lives they are capable of, not just the ones they think they are allowed to live.

I kept typing and slowly, the tension released from my body. At that moment, I knew I could finish the book.

The lived experience of this kind of "work" is so vastly different from what I did previously that I don't know how to compare the two. In the conventional workplace, I tried to be what others expected. But I was only able to find my good work by softening into myself. Now I embody an existence where the lines between work and non-work are dissolved. There is just living. This is why ideas like work-life balance or work-life integration are flawed. They wrongly assume that life can be partitioned into neat boxes and, more importantly, that everything we see as "work" can be covered in a job description.

When I talk about some of my challenges on this path, others respond skeptically. It's normal to complain about a "regular" job, but since I'm *choosing* my own path, the difficulties I deal with are seen as my fault. Of course, I agree! I cherish the responsibilities that come with existing outside of the system. But what most people miss are the profound benefits of this kind of existence. Time freedom, creative freedom, and time with my family are essential to what I feel is a full life. They are *everything* to me. But often, others can't "see" these things. Instead, they only see the prestige, status, and steady paycheck I've left behind. So if I mention that I'm uncertain about the next year on my path and others reply, "Just go back and get a job!" I want to shake them and say, "You don't get it! Uncertainty is such a small price to pay for this kind of life!"

Our culture convinces far too many of us to chase things that are not aligned with our ideal states of being. We internalize the message of what Byung-Chul Han has called the "achievement society" where the primary goal of a life is to constantly improve, nudged to become "entrepreneurs of [our]selves."[1] But constantly trying to be "better" can push us toward goals that are not ours, robbing us of our connection to ourselves.

This pressure makes it easy to overlook feelings of discontent. We tell ourselves that we should be grateful for our circumstances, especially once we've landed that "good" job. We dismiss stress, relationship challenges, long hours, or lack of personal time as trivial costs, necessary trade-offs we must make. Our focus shifts to the material outcomes that a job provides: the dream home, nice cars, and luxury vacations.

This creates an illusion. We start to identify more with our possessions than ourselves, convinced we can "have it all" no matter how we structure our work lives. Yet, deep down, we know this is a lie. I've talked with countless high-paid professionals in a state of low-grade misery, who ask me, "How do I find a new path without giving any of this up?"

The truth? I have absolutely no idea! Finding and doing good work almost always requires some sort of sacrifice. At a minimum, you must relinquish your job-based mindset and the belief that a job can deliver everything you desire out of life.

To me, the sacrifices I've made are worth it. *We have one life! Why spend it doing things you don't want to do?*

You might be able to keep the costs of your dissatisfaction at bay for years, but eventually your efforts to do so will wreak havoc on your life. To me, *this* is the greatest risk in the world. I know how hard it was to "recover" from years of cynical disinterest in my work. But now, I'm in the exact opposite position. I spend hardly any time doing work I'd rather skip and you'd have to make me an outrageous offer to consider going back.

From the outside, this is hard to understand and the path to good work often involves trade-offs that seem counterintuitive. For example, if I had more money, I might consider buying a house, but right now, Angie and

I are far happier having a cash cushion that allows us to "buy" time to work on creative projects, travel, and spend time with our daughter.[2] This decision can be baffling to people who take for granted that owning a home, especially once you have kids, is one of the primary goals of life. But we've spent a lot of time thinking about our values and the trade-offs we must make to live up to them. Sure, some people judge us for not embracing the same desires as the rest of society, but that's nothing compared to how we'd feel if we had to give up our good work and the life that it enables.

A life built around good work requires you to be brutally honest about what you truly want and what is actually possible. One of the hardest challenges I faced early on was that the work I had the most confidence in and my best way of making money, freelance consulting projects, was very clearly *not* my good work. Waking up to this realization took so long, however, because at one time I did love consulting work. During my first two years in the industry at McKinsey & Company, I was consistently challenged and inspired in a way similar to what I understand now as good work. But as the work got easier, my connection to the work faded. Rare moments when I felt creative and alive occurred mostly outside of work, like the informal career coaching I did in my friend circle, volunteering with first-generation college students, and writing on various blogs and social platforms. But those activities weren't "real work" worth noticing because they didn't generate money. It's clear now, however, that they offered something far more important: a sustainable energy that could fuel a different kind of life.

This is a crucial point: by worrying first and foremost about figuring out what people will pay for, too many people on the path toward good work short-circuit their own interests, curiosity, and energy. Instead of searching for skill-market fit, you should start with person-interest fit. *What are the activities you absolutely must do? What do you truly care about?* As the popular saying goes, "the reward for good work is more work," so you better like doing it!

But it can be incredibly hard to embrace the idea of surrendering to your work instead of putting money first, especially if you are still on a conventional path. A few years ago, I had a conversation with someone working at one of the big tech companies who enjoys writing. He hoped to write a book one day and told me that in another ten years, "once I have $10 million, I can quit and spend time with my family and write." At the time I was living in the Canary Islands with Angie, and over the previous twelve months I had probably earned just 10% of his income. I told him, "Well, that's what I'm doing now. I write most days, and hang out with my wife."

He countered, "Well, I want to stay in luxury resorts and have access to concierge nannies. I don't want to sacrifice anything for my family."

Because I love seeing people come alive and do the work that matters to them, I wanted to convince him that he might accomplish his financial goal but lose connection to his creative capacity in the process. On my previous path I did not pay attention to the hidden, creeping costs of being completely disconnected from what brought me alive. It's shocking how long it took me to reawaken my inner ambition, drive, and creative spirit after quitting my job. In *The Pathless Path*, I argued that "the longer you spend on a path that isn't yours, the longer it takes you to find one that is."[3] I believe this even more strongly now as I still find myself shedding some of the baggage of my previous path. I don't think I changed his mind, but I sure hope he can quit his job and write his book when he hits his financial goal. Honestly, I suspect it's going to be a bit harder and take a bit longer than he thinks.

I've found over and over again that the people most afraid to leave their jobs are similar to the tech employee I talked with: well-compensated, Type A achievers. They are not limited by their own capacity for action or their financial situation. Instead, they are constrained by their assumptions that life revolves around continuous employment and a steady career trajectory. On top of this, they are surrounded by others in similar situations, who collectively agree that tolerating a job you dislike is less risky than wandering without a goal in search of something better.

Even as fears keep people in jobs they don't enjoy, fleeting moments of good work can offer temporary hope, delaying real change. At the Boston Consulting

Group (BCG), I experienced this while working closely with my manager, Omeed, on a practice strategy redesign. For two intense months, we were absorbed in the work. It rekindled a sense of connection I'd felt years earlier as a volunteer organizer for the Sloan Sports Analytics Conference in grad school. By the end of the project, I craved more — but then Omeed left the company, and I found myself reassigned to my third manager in less than a year. This marked my third straight year of never working with the same people for more than six months. Yet, my brief experience with Omeed injected me with a temporary optimism. I convinced myself that I just hadn't yet found the right job.

It's clear now that much of the frantic job-hopping during my twenties was motivated by much more than wanting my managers to stick around. It was a desperate search for good work. Deep down, I craved being challenged. An inner ambition still burned inside of me and while my experiences were trying to convince me it wasn't possible, I never gave up hope.

Having many jobs has exposed me to a wide range of work experiences. At General Electric, in my first job, I mindlessly compiled data on aircraft engine parts. No one cared if I knew anything about the business or the accounting principles we used. All that mattered was using the right colors, font size, and formatting that the Vice President expected. Most people can easily recognize this kind of soul-draining work, but in some jobs it is more difficult to spot. In conversations with people who burned out after landing dream jobs in corporate sustainability or non-profits, I saw people grapple with the dissonance between their deep desire to have an "impact" and the harsh realities and opposing pressures of the organizations in which they found themselves.

Many people working in "helping" professions, such as therapists, nurses, and doctors, often struggle with the even greater confusion of having jobs that do contain good work. However, this work is often only a small part of their days. For example, I've talked to several doctors who explain how much they love their work with patients but are deflated by insurance company requirements, ever-changing metrics, internal politics, and endless new initiatives. In effect, a doctor's job undermines the doctor's good work.

So many professionals accept this type of work arrangement as the best they can hope for, convincing themselves that work is not meant to be enjoyed. In fields like consulting, finance, and law, this situation is even normalized and many people enter these careers *expecting* to make sacrifices in their lives before they start. "I'll just give up two years of my life, then I'll do what I really want" people tell themselves. This is incredibly risky because if you stay too long, you get lulled into accepting that the low-grade dissatisfaction associated with doing a job is not worth questioning; it's just proof that you're human.

Orienting adulthood around full-time employment is

a rather new invention in the arc of human history. Yet, we have a hard time thinking there is any other way to spend our lives, convinced that a well-paying, "good" job is the center of a life well lived. But if you are like me, you see this as one option of many. You are reading this book because you want more. You feel with every bone in your body that the frustration is no longer worth it and you are willing to make sacrifices to search for something deeper.

Engaging in this quest became far easier for me when I decoupled the idea of "work" from the idea of a "job." Without this constraint, I can take my work more seriously and less seriously at the same time. I can both prioritize the work that matters to me and remain detached from what that work says about me as a person. If I have to do a short stint doing paid work or a job I don't enjoy, so be it. It wouldn't mean that I am not succeeding on my current path, but merely taking a detour on my lifelong journey of building a life around good work.

After I quit my consulting job and started tapping into the energy of good work, I noticed that both this way of working and the energy it gave me were largely invisible, if not unimaginable, to others. As I started to develop a better relationship with work, some friends and family members still asked questions like, "What's your plan for making money?" "Are you really not going to get a job again?"

In response, all I could think was "Holy shit, I've

found something that is so fulfilling and makes me feel so alive, and yet no one even knows that this way of living is possible!?!"

Why weren't people asking me, "Have you found work that has lit a fire in your soul?"

So I'll just ask you instead, *What's lighting a fire in your soul?*

7
QUESTION YOUR WORK SCRIPTS

For the first ten years of my career, I was unknowingly an actor in a grand production called "work." My role was to act out the scripts in my head, some of my own creation and others absorbed from the culture around me.

The scripts were powerful. They told me that "work" and "a job" are the same thing and that work is the center of life. They convinced me that no breaks were allowed: you must work non-stop from graduation to retirement. And since you can't avoid work, the best approach is to find something tolerable, and more importantly, well-paid. Based on how much people talked about money, nothing else seemed relevant. *"Social work? Don't do that, you'll be poor!"* *"Engineers have the best starting salaries!"* *"Did you hear how much Chad is making working on Wall Street?"*

These stories are useful. They gave me important information about some of the real constraints of the modern world and what material life outcomes are possible based on what kinds of work I pursued. But they also narrowed my imagination. When I walked away from my job, suddenly having to improvise on a pathless path, I became aware of a vast world beyond the paycheck reality I had inhabited. I was without a script. Unmoored. I had to write my own story.

As I leaned into things like writing in the first couple of years of self-employment, it challenged everything I knew about work. I definitely felt the pressure to make money from writing and to turn it into a job, making it a "legitimate" way to spend my time. But I rejected this impulse. When people asked what I was "working on," I would say, "I'm just having fun exploring ideas and seeing where they take me." I refused to call any of it work. Work was formal employment, something you got paid for. Work couldn't be fun, let alone as joyous as writing. *Right?* But I couldn't find a better word. And so here we are, seven chapters into this book, and I have already used the word "work" more than 250 times. But this is intentional. *Good Work* is my attempt to reclaim the word "work" from its common meaning in the broader culture and to use it to rewrite my own story. Work does not have to be something we must endure. It is a vital part of the human experience, something that makes us feel good.

Each of us grows up with a collection of stories and scripts about work that we inherit from our culture, family, and friends. These scripts point us in certain directions and mold our desires for what we want to do in the world. Many scripts are helpful, telling us how the world works, but others can hold us back.

On my podcast, for the last couple of years I've been opening up every interview with this question: "What are the stories and scripts you grew up with around work?" In almost every case, people explain how their scripts shaped their reality and then how they had to unlearn these scripts as they went through shifts in their lives. Their responses all share a similarity. They are clear and definitive scripts one can follow. They say, *"You don't have to worry, this is how life works."*

I've simplified this collection of scripts down to a list of common stories about work that people adopt when they are young. Look through the list and simply notice how you feel. *Do you agree with this? Does it make you angry? Do you disagree?* Just notice your reactions.

- "Anything worthwhile requires suffering."
- "Put school and work above everything else."
- "Work is a way to express your gifts."
- "A man must sacrifice to earn money for the family."
- "People who do harder things are better people."
- "Full-time jobs are not safe."
- "If you don't work hard, you'll run out of money."
- "Work hard and you'll be rewarded."

- "Stable jobs are good jobs."
- "You should be grateful to have a job."
- "Entrepreneurship is risky."
- "You can do whatever you want. Follow your dreams."
- "Graduate from college and then you don't have to worry."
- "Secure the highest paying job possible."
- "You can be your best self at work."
- "Starting your own business is the only way to be sovereign."
- "Always aim to succeed and climb that ladder."
- "You work because you have to."
- "You can play once the work is done."
- "Work can be joyous."
- "The best thing you can do with your life is work where you can have an impact."
- "Have fun, sure. But then settle down, get serious, and get a stable job."

As you read through this list, you likely had strong reactions. Through this exercise, people often become aware of the hidden assumptions and scripts they have about how the world is supposed to operate, especially when it comes to work. What's striking is how these scripts vary from person to person. This shows us they are not fixed realities, but stories we can rewrite.

When a friend told me that his parents encouraged

him to find work that felt joyous, I was a bit shocked. *What if I had grown up with that idea?* In a world where many people expect to work 80,000 hours in adulthood, I've been surprised at how little time people spend thinking about the stories and scripts they attach to work. In the search for good work, this sort of contemplation is vital. The questions I most often come back to include:

- *What is work?*
- *How did you arrive at that conclusion?*
- *What scripts are you unconsciously living out?*
- *Are they serving you or holding you back?*
- *Is there a better script for your life, right now?*

These questions have helped me gain a deeper understanding of the decisions I've made and how I might still be limiting the possibilities of my life. Being in a relationship with Angie has made this contemplation even more important and helped me reflect on my assumptions about work *and* life much more regularly. Growing up in two distinctly different countries and cultures, we often have radically different assumptions about how to approach the same situation. When Angie and I were first dating, we talked about many of our own stories. She grew up hearing the phrase, "We're not the kind of people that earn money, so you need to learn how to fit in and work." This script may seem harsh, but it may have been useful in the past: her parents grew up in Taiwan during a period of rapid industrialization and workers had very few rights. Her family didn't have as many economic opportunities as she has now, so the script served some purpose. But when we moved to the U.S. and Angie had access to the American labor market, she still wanted to charge just $5 an hour for her work. I nudged her to consider retiring some of the stories that she absorbed growing up in Taiwan.

But letting go of scripts is hard. Questioning these stories can be unsettling because they are often tied to moral values prized by the cultures we grew up in. From an early age, many people are raised to make judgments about others based on what kinds of work they do, how they do it, and how much money they make. Through this, we learn to judge ourselves even more harshly. In the U.S., for example, there is a widespread negative reaction to anyone who does not seem to be doing their fair share of work. We even create elaborate government systems to ensure that people don't get handouts too easily. Through that lens, as I decided to work less and make less money, I was a worthless layabout destined to live a life of self-imposed poverty. Although I wanted to stay on this path, I still subconsciously saw my previous path as the "better" path. "Good" people remain employed and people without a good work ethic are not to be trusted. Recognizing these ingrained beliefs and understanding their impact on me was important. Realizing they weren't universal truths helped me gradually release the shame I felt by violating them. This took time but was vital in improving my relationship with work.

Given how much work I've done to understand my own relationship to work, I now see people's work scripts show up everywhere. In 2023, Vox published an article which jumped off the page at me titled "How some people get away with doing nothing at work." It described several people "getting away" with working less at their full-time jobs. The article opens with Nate, who "[i]n theory... works 40 hours a week in the operations department at a major fintech company." But "in reality, Nate works one hour a day at most."[1]

In another example, Bobby "spends his day doing research and development for his own tech projects. When he doesn't feel like doing anything, he goes hiking or swimming or plays video games and watches movies. He gets to spend more time with his kids." Bobby recounts his work experience: "It's like being on vacation all the time, with occasional scrambling to do a thing, then doing the thing for a couple of hours, then going back to the rest of my life." Bobby's made a little better use of his time than Nate, but he still has to orient his life around being available for the "occasional scrambling."

These stories are entertaining, but what especially stood out was the author's comment: ***"What was most surprising was that many did not exactly love the situation."*** Seen through the lens of good work, I completely disagree. This is not surprising at all! Both of these work situations sound great on paper – working "one hour a day at most" or "it's like being on vacation" – but you couldn't pay me any amount of money to trade places with Nate or Bobby. After quitting my job, I was shocked at how much time I had wasted at work. I started valuing my time much more and it helped me make sacrifices to preserve it. Many people go through a similar "repricing" of their time after transitioning to something better. Before I quit my job, I saw taking a pay cut as a foolish act. But after experiencing the joy and possibility associated with work I do on my own terms, I realized that I had sold my time too cheaply and for too long. Now that I have tasted this freedom, I will not be soul-sucked for any amount of money.

During my twenties, however, my soul was very much for sale. At the same time, I clawed at the edges of my work life for freedom. My version of "work-life balance" involved taking every single vacation day, leaving work at 3pm on Fridays, never working too late, and working remotely as much as possible. But despite not working crazy hours, I was still immersed in a "career-first" identity. I thought that the relative freedom allowed by a "good" job was the best possible outcome for my life.

In consulting, I had many stretches similar to Nate's, without much to do. This is a normal part of client service. We even used the phrase "on the beach" to describe people who were not working on a client project. While you could do whatever you wanted during these stretches, you were still encouraged to work on internal projects and make appearances at the office. Being "on the beach" sounds great, too, until you realize that in return, when you are actively working on a client project, the client's needs come before everything else in your life. This resulted in a weird balance: no one cared if you were at the gym on a random Tuesday, but if you were staffed on a project and the client started having a tantrum at 7pm on a Saturday, you were expected to be ready to work. You are like an on-call doctor, paid to be available for emergencies, but instead of saving lives, you perform last minute surgery on PowerPoint decks. A lot of knowledge work is highly paid exactly because of this demand uncertainty. You are paid to be "on the clock."

And this is what drives people in these jobs mad, because it feels like you can't escape. You double-down on trying to make the work more meaningful or you look for ways to work less. You repurpose your inherent creativity to figure out how to escape the nonsense, exploit the system, or extract as much money from the company as possible. In one of my jobs, for months at a time I would have just five to ten hours of client work a week, but I was still expected to commute and be in the office for more than 55 hours a week. I literally did laps around the office, drank extra coffee just to feel something, and took two-hour lunches in the park, sometimes taking a nap on the grass. That might sound like "getting away with doing nothing," but to me it was worse than being busy because I was constantly aware of the fact that I was not free.

In 2022, a series of labor market reports triggered a collective panic around what media outlets were calling the "great resignation." It culminated in a headline in The New York Times that February proclaiming "The Age of Anti-Ambition."[2] The article included accounts of people who wanted to escape toxic situations in the workplace and claimed that these stories provided proof of a movement *against* ambition.

But what if rejecting performative busy work is one of the most ambitious things a human can do? For a long time, the word "ambition" has been connected with the pursuit of external success, starting from its derivation from the Latin *ambitio*, which described the act of Roman politicians soliciting votes, or seeking external approval. But we don't have to accept this definition today. We can reclaim the word "ambition" by using it to refer to our deeper desires, something author Luke Burgis has called our "thick desires." As Burgis says, "thick desires are like these layers of rock that have been built up throughout the course of our lives. These are desires that can be shaped and cultivated through models like our parents and people that we admire as children. But at some level, they're related to the core of who we are."[3] For too long, ambition has been thought of as something that aims outward. It's time to repurpose this word, making it part of the search for good work, which requires us to go inward.

This approach is already becoming more popular with young people such as Arjun Khemani, a 17-year-old high school dropout from India. Listening to his conversation with Jim O'Shaughnessy on the *Infinite Loops* podcast, I was intrigued by the apparent ease with which Arjun rejected one of the work scripts that had taken me so long to question. He told Jim, "Hard work is overrated," explaining that "all of these successful and well-achieved people talk about how much hard work they had to put in and how much they had to sacrifice, but I think it's just way more creative and productive to follow your interests and to just see where they lead you."[4]

I recoiled initially when I heard Arjun so confidently reject something so sacred as the phrase "hard work." *Can he just say that?* But then I realized he was saying something much more important. He wasn't rejecting "hard work," he was rejecting the industrial-era belief that you need to "pay your dues" and slowly climb a corporate ladder. His version of ambition was going after what he cares about, right now. He's involved in multiple startups, learning several skills, and building a network of friends and supporters through his podcast and the internet. He's walking the walk and following his interests, full out. More than twenty years my junior, Arjun's story is a good reminder for me too, that work's role in our lives and the stories we tell about it will continue to evolve. His reflections gave me hope that more people can shift away from the "work is pain" story that was handed down from previous generations and toward one where work can be a powerful container that aligns us not only with the possibilities of our time, but our own unique interests.

I wish I had questioned my own stories when I was younger because it would have enabled me to find and commit to good work earlier. One of those stories I told myself was that I was driven and successful, but not as ambitious as the people around me. I was always somewhat amazed at the people who were fully engaged in their jobs and pursued promotions and raises with their entire life force. After I quit my consulting job, I was shocked at how much some of these scripts limited the possibilities of my life. Questioning and rewriting them took time, but once I did, it was as if I stepped into a new reality filled with far more abundance and possibility.

You have a choice: you can accept the scripts you grew up with that tell you what a successful work life looks like, or you can author new ones. Life isn't a single movie script that everyone should perform identically, it's something we must improvise.

What is the most ambitious path for you? Is there a script for it yet? Or do you need to write your own too?

PART THREE
EMBRACE THE CHALLENGES

"In a way, work is like a love affair. It demands commitment, absorption, and care."[1]

— VIRGINIA VALIAN

"Good work and good education are achieved by visitation and then absence, appearance and disappearance. Most people who exhibit a mastery in a work or a subject have often left it completely for a long period in their lives only to return for another look. Constant busyness has no absence in it, no openness to the arrival of any new season, no birdsong at the start of its day. Constant learning is counterproductive and makes both ourselves and the subject stale and uninteresting."[2]

— DAVID WHYTE

8

SOLVE THE PUZZLE OF
GOOD WORK

After I quit my job and stopped trying to do things I didn't enjoy, I discovered a massive reserve of energy. Now, I treat that energy like an endurance athlete: carefully pacing myself so that I can continue on this path. If burnout means running out of energy to keep going, then managing my energy is a top priority. This requires maintaining a subtle balance among the various kinds of work I do:

- **Good work:** activities that give me energy and fuel my journey
- **"Good enough" work:** tasks I enjoy to some degree, which often help pay the bills, but are not my core good work
- **Supporting activities:** complementary work that supports my good work, but is sometimes a distraction

- **"Bad" work:** work I seek to avoid. Anything that drains my energy, but sometimes necessary to pay the bills.

Embracing this "puzzle of good work" means accepting that these elements are always in flux, and that while a certain schedule or structure might work right now, it may shift in the future. I'm grateful that Angie and I had several years to experiment with how we spend our time before having kids. It helped us understand that building a life around good work is not supposed to be easy: it requires constant tinkering, reflection, and patience.

In today's world, remote and gig work provide more opportunities than ever to work flexibly. This is a great addition to the range of work options that people searching for good work need to consider. I've been able to piece together what is essentially a part-time job from selling a digital product, facilitating virtual workshops, and various other gigs. This enables me to think about writing with a long-term mindset, allowing me to take creative risks, avoid short-term trade-offs and maintain creative autonomy.

This has required discipline. When I started blogging before I quit my job, people asked if I was planning to write a book. Not because they thought it might be an enjoyable creative challenge, but because they knew that writers make money doing it. These people shared the assumption I had made for years, that any work worth doing *must* come with a paycheck.

However, rushing to directly monetize your good work can be a mistake. The right approach is to treat the work that feels good as sacred, protecting it as long as possible by making money doing something else. There are many famous stories of people doing this. Whether it be Albert Einstein working at a patent office, the poet Wallace Stevens at an insurance company, or the author Harper Lee in airline reservations, there is an endless list of people that go out of their way to protect the work that matters to them.

After committing to my good work, I consciously set out to separate it from not only my identity, but also my monetization strategy for as long as possible. The composer Philip Glass took a similar approach, and shared why he drove a taxi early in his career to support his musical life: "It was the quickest and easiest way to make an honest living. I thought it was a pretty good deal. I didn't have to teach any classes anywhere. I just drove the car and I got paid. I liked that. I had my independence, which was very important to me."[1]

The notion that jumps out is "independence." I've approached my writing with a similar spirit. Instead of making money from my good work, I've focused on the much more lucrative StrategyU platform that Jay convinced me to double down on in Bali. While I've probably made less money than I could have if I focused on it full-time, I've been able to keep it running with about 15-20 hours of effort each month and it has helped give me a "basic income" that lets me approach my writing with complete independence. This demands a clear stance on which work I should actually be doing. In this spirit, I've been deliberate in automating or ignoring the parts of StrategyU I don't enjoy and spending more time doing what I find rewarding, like writing material for the site that drives traffic to the course and thinking through how to synthesize the ideas to teach them in a virtual environment.

Over time, these efforts led to requests from companies to deliver training for their teams. At first, I resisted, not wanting to work for big companies again, but decided it was worth a test. I realized that I could create a package that fit my life and tell potential clients, "This is what I will do, take it or leave it." While it wasn't my good work, I found these projects far more enjoyable than the consulting projects I had done previously. As I gained confidence, I raised prices, and I've been able to do a couple of these workshops each year, "buying" time to focus on writing afterward. Despite sometimes losing motivation for writing when I'm in the midst of these projects, I'm usually able to shift back to writing quickly. If I had all the money in the world, would I still do the consulting workshops? Probably not. But I don't resent this "good enough" work: it's a pragmatic and somewhat aligned way to keep going on this path.

Each project taught me more about the subtle balance between money, time, and my own motivation–a useful skill upon having a child, when I had to restructure my approach to work. Four months after Michelle's birth, I resumed my casual approach to writing, but struggled to find any sense of flow as I was now prioritizing family. Nine months in, frustrated with my lack of progress, and the irresistible distraction of my daughter's presence, I realized I needed a complete shift in how I was thinking about work. I had always prided myself on focusing at home easily, but now, I had to consider working elsewhere for the first time. Beyond this, I questioned many of the supporting activities that complemented my writing, like podcasting, conversations, and reading. *Were they really serving my work or were they just distractions?* Such activities often give people energy but it's easy to mistake them for your good work. My podcast is enjoyable and something that allows me to discover and play with ideas, but I know it is *not* my good work. If I prioritize it over writing, things start to feel off. This understanding helps me take action to pause things like my podcast, newsletter, and coffee chats whenever I sense I need to reconnect with my good work.

Managing this way of working is fundamentally different from succeeding on a traditional path. Instead of optimizing your time, you optimize your energy and pay attention to how you feel over time. Most of the world defaults instead to a factory schedule. They see work as constant effort. Five days per week, eight hours per day. However, my experiments with writing and work over the years have helped me see how limiting this perspective is. How much great work is never started because of people's dedication to the standard work-week? I love considering questions like this. I mean, what if writing a masterpiece would require taking an entire year off followed by a year of intense work? Or that the best work might result from working in seasons, taking every fourth month off? Working on my own, focused on staying connected to my good work, these questions aren't frivolous, they are necessary.

A helpful reframe for me has been expanding the timescale from workdays and workweeks to "work months" and "work years." Through this lens I notice natural "seasons" in my work. Whether it's six-week sprints to finish a draft, or a three-month period of explosive ideation, or a two-month stretch where I experiment and build an online course, whenever I leave space open for these shifts and then ride the wave of energy, good things tend to happen.

With writing, I've adopted the mantra of "write, most days." Writing doesn't deplete me and usually even gives me energy. But it's a delicate balance. If I wrote for twelve hours a day for weeks, I would end up depleted. If you observe me on any given day, you might think I never work. But if you zoom out and see my consistency and production over a number of years, it's impressive: hundreds of newsletters and blog posts, thousands of social media posts, and now, two books. Experimenting with the mix of activities and my schedule is time consuming, but it is also hugely rewarding. Since I'm committed to building my life around good work, "wasting" days, weeks, or even months experimenting with new schedules is not a big deal. The real risk is wasting *years* working on the wrong things. When I find the right flow with my work, my life is effortless and full.

After struggling with our unstructured approach after having a baby, Angie and I realized we needed to consider other options if we were going to finish our books. We reluctantly embraced a structured workweek, something we had rejected for years. Now, we alternate between personal work days and childcare in a four- or five-day workweek. While there's tons of flexibility in our setup to support each other as parents, I've found tremendous energy in knowing that every week my schedule includes writing blocks that I will not compromise for anything. While I still write at random times, these "schedule anchors'" have allowed me to find a sense of flow over a series of days and weeks that feels good. When I'm in this state, something like a book takes over my life in the best way possible, and my life becomes injected with a sense of meaning and satisfaction. I don't have to push to complete it and instead, I am pulled forward. This is how I experience good work, and to me, it's absolutely delightful.

Most people who have found a powerful relationship with a certain kind of work are fiercely determined to protect it at all costs. Ted Gioia, a writer and former consultant himself, described his own long-term commitment to writing in a conversation with David

Perell on the *How I Write* podcast. Ted was *not* willing to make some of the sacrifices that I have for his good work. As he told David, "I was going to earn a living. I was going to have a good family life. I was going to live where I want to." [2] So for many years, he remained employed. The sacrifice he made was sleep. He would get up at 5:30am to read and pursue his own self-directed education before he did his money-making work. He spent time reading and listening to music, things that inspired his writing. As he reflected, "People view me as a writer and I am a writer, I'm a productive writer, but I don't start writing until the afternoon. The whole morning is devoted to listening to music and reading and mostly reading books." What jumped out to me was a comment that signaled how seriously he took this good work: "I did not do this as a career strategy. I didn't do this to make money or anything."

People who have found their good work, like Ted, feel that they *must* make it work. They sharpen their focus on what matters to them and which trade-offs they are willing to make, and then they do their work wholeheartedly. But these commitments rarely happen without support. Without Angie, I don't think anything I've done would have been possible. At every step of the way, despite my doubts or insecurities, she encourages me to keep going. And when I tell her that I'd go back and get a job if necessary to meet our needs, she typically rolls her eyes, signaling that she is willing to sacrifice anything to help me avoid that fate. My friend, Rick

Lewis, a speaker and performer, recounted a similar story after finding himself without work after the global financial crisis in 2009. With a third child on the way, he felt pressured to make money and told his wife he was planning a pivot into web design. But, as Rick says, "when I shared this idea with my wife, she surprisingly – and fiercely – forbade it. 'You are NOT a web designer,' she insisted."[3] Reminders like this from people we trust can be powerful motivators to keep going on our existing paths despite the doubts and uncertainties.

Solving the puzzle of good work is something I happily embrace because when I left my job, I knew I didn't want to recreate the conditions I left behind. Before quitting, I spent three years working after recovering from health challenges. I went through my days sharply aware of how my environment made me feel. By the end of those three years, I couldn't take it anymore. I felt stuck, trapped, and disillusioned. In my last job, it was as if I was carrying a 50 pound backpack filled with sand through my days. For one project, I spent months going to meetings to prepare for meetings to prepare for other meetings where people decided to just keep having meetings. It was intolerable, but I am grateful for this and other similar experiences. It is a visceral reminder of what I don't want to return to, and it helps me stay attuned to how I feel doing different kinds of work. When I experience the same feeling I had in those endless meetings, I know I'm about to work on something that will send me in the wrong direction.

But we inevitably make mistakes. Before I took the consulting project in Thailand, I wasn't feeling good about it. But I overrode my intuition with my rational spreadsheet calculations and traded short-term energy for a long-term payoff. After that, I implemented several "gating" criteria to determine if the work I am considering is right for me. One of my favorite filters is "How much would I pay to work on this?" It flips the frame from working for money to paying for the right to work. When I ask this question, very little work other than writing passes the test. Generally, doing something now that might result in freedom *later* is almost always a red flag. It's easy to keep telling yourself that "someday" you will do the important work you care about. There's always more money to earn or more preparation needed. To override this impulse, I try to jump to that imagined future state when everything will be "okay" and ask myself how I can embody that state, right now.

Making these decisions is hard. The path to good work is filled with uncertainty. This is because your path will be uniquely yours and the challenges you face will be one-of-a-kind. No one else can take the path you will take. While others can support you and offer guidance, no one will ever fully understand what you are doing and where you are headed. To deal with this confusing sense of lostness, it is tempting to follow other's paths or embrace strong identities and labels. Sometimes I feel the pull to embrace labels like "CEO of a Training Firm," or "Published Author," or even the recently popular

"Creator." While I may use these labels in a pragmatic sense in conversations and even sometimes in formal bios, I reject them as a way to see myself completely. I don't write for awards or for financial rewards. I am not a Writer; *I simply write.* I write because I enjoy it and it matters to me. Identifying too closely with a specific work identity narrows my imagination and creates artificial constraints that are unnecessary. The book writing may be the "sexiest" thing I do, but I am *all* of the work I do, including the "bad" work I must sometimes do to pay the bills. Despite this, people often demand that you use labels. I've found it freeing to adopt ambiguous ones like "curious human" which don't come with a prescribed work path.

When you embrace the puzzle of good work, you become attuned to how everything in your life fits together. You become the conductor of your life, trying to balance all the different "notes" to create a sense of harmony. You become aware of the conversations you have, the things you consume, the amount of exercise you do, your environment, and the people you spend time with. Having a child has sharpened my attention even further, helping me understand how fragile this balance of activities can be.

For me, searching for, finding, and then protecting my good work is rewarding because when I am anchored in activities that give me energy, everything else in my life improves. However, on this path you will inevitably lose connection to what matters and have to find it again.

Yet the ongoing quest becomes easier over time because the more times you lose your way and then come back to center, the more confidence and determination you'll have to keep going. And that type of determination is one of the most powerful forces in the world.

With time, most of the things we work on in our lives will fade from memory. When I look back on my twenties, it's hard to remember much of what I did while on the clock. But when I recall the early days of writing around the world and the year I spent working on my first book, those memories seem to get richer with time. I cherish those moments. And this is what we're trying to do with our lives anyway, right? Do things that matter to us and look back on our actions with satisfaction and joy. This is why continuing to solve the puzzle of good work is worth it.

To inject this perspective into what I do now, I ask myself these three questions with regard to anything I'm working on. The questions might help you, too:

1. Looking back, what chunks of time feel satisfying and seem to be more important as time progresses?
2. What am I drawn to do, right now? What am I doing already that feels good?
3. At the end of my life, what will I definitely not regret having done?

The puzzle of good work is a puzzle that will never

fully be "solved." These questions, however, can help orient us to the present and remind us of the good work that we are meant to be doing. We can never be quite sure that we are spending our time in the ways that will be most meaningful to us, but most people are keenly aware of what they should definitely *not* be working on. If we take the puzzle of good work seriously and protect the activities which matter most to us, at the end of this one wild and crazy life, we'll think, *Yeah, that was nice.*

9
DO WHAT FEELS RIGHT

Working on something you enjoy at a leisurely pace can have shockingly good results over a long period of time, even though it goes against how most work is done in the modern world. My approach, which I've even jokingly coined the "long, slow, stupid, fun way" works well because I stay hyper-aware of what I'm actually interested in doing. I ask myself the question, "What if I went slower?" to remember that despite there being an abundance of "best practices" and tactics to accelerate growth in almost everything I do, that is not my goal. It is simply to stay in the game and remain connected to my good work. You can go fast to win the race, but I am trying to go slow in order to go far. While this may make me feel "stupid," in that I am consciously rejecting proven ways of succeeding, my approach works for me. At every point, I am intentionally directing my time and attention and rarely feel out of control. I stay connected to what matters, seldom wasting time on work I regret doing, and when opportunities emerge, I have the space in my life to take action.

It took me fourteen months to write *The Pathless Path*, and the entire process felt light and enjoyable. When I started, I benefited from years of developing a relationship with writing and a humble appreciation of the rhythms that help produce my best work. I was also able to quickly orient my life around a book project because I had been slow and cautious to commit to anything else. In the year before I started the book, my calendar rarely had meetings. Each day, I would wake up without much of a plan. I let my curiosity guide me, spending lots of time reading, thinking, and writing about work.

During the pandemic in 2020, my writing hit a chord. Working remotely and forced to slow down, people were looking for answers to their existential questions, ones I had been obsessed with for the past few years. I followed my curiosity and became even more deeply absorbed in my thinking and writing. That entire year I was in the zone, having conversations with people from around the world and sharing and writing about what I learned each week in my newsletter. I loved it.

At the end of the year, Angie and I moved to Puerto Escondido, Mexico for three months, once again following my friend Jonny to a beautiful beach town. Within one week near the end of 2020, I had conversations with multiple people strongly urging me to write a book. Many had told me this over the years, but now it was multiple people within a single week. I remember one person clearly saying, *"You've written so much, I wish I could just read it in book form!"* It stuck with me. As I wandered around the beach town, I couldn't stop thinking about it. I was more than three years into my self-employment journey and I had been optimizing for spending time with Angie and traveling over the previous two years. It felt like a good opportunity to trade my freedom for a chance to deepen my commitment to my good work.

I decided I would just start. I opened a Word document one morning at the kitchen table and put all my writing and ideas into a single document. I started organizing everything into a high-level table of contents. I got lost in the document for a couple of hours and as I snapped out of it, I noticed it was almost lunchtime. I walked outside to the patio where Jonny was working on the wooden standing desk he had commissioned from a local woodworker, and said, "I think it's time to do a book."

"Hell, yeah," he replied.

I laughed and said, "I guess it's happening."

For the next two months, I kept working on the document. The more time I spent, the more excited I became. It felt right. I was pushing the edge on my skills and I happily let the process take over my life.

Writing the book sharpened my awareness of my relationship to writing. *Did I write better in the morning or at night? Did I do better work when I wrote every day or when I took breaks?* As the book absorbed my thinking, it became a powerful filter for my curiosity, too. Everything around me became something that might fit into the book. I started to see writing as a sacred act, one with its own wisdom. I didn't dare override the natural flow of ideas and words moving between my mind and the page. Some days I'd write for thirty minutes and feel stuck. Then I'd stand up and declare I was done for the day. On other days, I'd get completely lost in flow for hours, fully enjoying the process. I was trusting my intuition and following my energy.

When I noticed how good ideas seemed to emerge if I stopped writing for a couple of days or went for long walks, I decided to experiment further. I declared every seventh week a "leisure week." When the Friday of the sixth week came around, I stopped writing and didn't do any kind of work for another week. During those "weeks off" I would wander, go hiking with Angie, ride my bike, read, and pay attention. My mind often overflowed with ideas, and I definitely jotted down notes, but I resisted any temptation to write. When I returned to writing the following Monday, ideas overflowed. Those weeks of contemplation and rest quietly shaped the heart of my book, revealing that sometimes, the most productive thing to do is nothing at all.

In the beginning of 2022, I was nearing completion of the book. Lying on my bed in Austin, Texas, where we had just moved into an apartment a week earlier, I did a final read-through on my Kindle. As I finished, I sat up and walked into the living room. I declared to Angie, "It's done. I did it!" Now I had to get it out into the world. For months I had known that I wasn't interested in doing a months-long launch for the book because every time I started researching best practices, all I wanted to do was go back to writing. So when I was ready, I gathered everything and submitted the files to the various publishing platforms. On the ebook version, I decided on a three-week pre-sale. As I uploaded the paperback version, I noticed there was no such option. *Weird.* The next morning I woke up to an email, "Your book is for sale." *Shit.* I re-read the email and confirmed, my book was now live across the world. I had overlooked the fact that Amazon's KDP platform didn't allow pre-sales for paperbacks. I laughed to myself and quickly updated my plan. I opened Substack and wrote a short post letting people know it was for sale. A friend later told me that he was dumbfounded: "I couldn't believe you seriously just launched your book with one post." But to me, the project was already a success. The book had transformed me, pushing me beyond what I thought I was capable of, and I couldn't wait to send it to friends. Selling tons of copies was never the goal. This may shock people, but it's true. The only intention was to write something I wanted to write and to deepen my commitment to writing. Writing is my good work, not book launches.

After the book was out in the world, I spent the next two months working on a consulting project. Because I didn't expect to sell that many books and we had just moved back to the U. S., the $25,000 I was offered to work on the project was too much to turn down. But during one call with a C-level executive in which he tried to make me feel small, I was reminded once again of why I had moved away from this kind of work. It was the first project like this I had taken since I had sworn them off in Bali three years earlier. But like I said, we all make mistakes. Even me, one more time. It was another helpful nudge from the universe to double down on my good work.

I asked myself what kind of approach would both feel good *and* inspire me to continue writing and exploring ideas about work. I realized that my "curiosity conversations" had played a major role in shaping the ideas that led to the book. Over the previous few years I had done hundreds of these conversations with strangers from around the world, along with over 100 podcast interviews, all on the topic of work. I decided to double down on my podcast, renaming it from *Reimagine Work* to *The Pathless Path Podcast*, actively embracing the phrase and becoming more comfortable sharing it.

In some ways, this is backward. Most people try to spend all their time going on *other people's* podcasts to promote their book. But I realized that I'd get a lot more energy out of continuing to talk about the ideas with people on my own show, at my own pace. By leaning into this way of showing up into the world, I started to bring forth my genuine ambition and as I pushed my own comfort zone on sharing my work and ideas, I could see others get excited too. Book sales started to accelerate soon after and I could feel something special starting to happen. It was clear what I had to do: stay connected to my excitement and curiosity.

Another method of sharing that felt good involved experiments with the gift economy. I decided to give away *The Pathless Path* to anyone who wanted it. In the first two years, I gifted thousands of physical books and thousands more of the digital version. I even developed a playful new spin on these giveaways, which I called "guerrilla gifting." I left hundreds of books in airports, parks, and little libraries, and on stoops, paths, and park benches around the world with a note saying that the book was a gift from the author. Not expecting anything in return, I have enjoyed getting random messages from people across the globe who reach out after finding a book and reading it. Many authors recoil at the idea of giving their work away, but I love it because not only am I distributing my book and my ideas, but I'm having more fun along the way. It's the only marketing that "feels right" to me.

I constantly remind myself, writing is my good work, something I want to protect from worldly, money-making pressures as long as possible. But in that first year of the book's life, I was emboldened by the dozens of emails I received from readers. People sent me messages like, "Your book changed my life," and "I finally feel good about my current path." I thought to myself, "*Wow, people really do love this book!*" Every email I received boosted my confidence. I sensed I had an opportunity to be more ambitious in promoting it without losing myself in the process.

I became even bolder. I sent the book to people with large audiences and invited some of my dream guests like Russ Roberts, Kevin Kelly, and Derek Sivers onto my podcast. People seemed to feed off my genuine enthusiasm and things started to snowball. Ali Abdaal, a YouTuber with a large audience, shared a video about my book on his channel that reached more than half a million people. Sales accelerated, and I ended up selling more than 35,000 copies of the book in my second year, more than three times as many as in the first year.

Penguin Random House, one of the leading publishing houses, noticed the increasing sales. They approached me and within a couple of weeks offered me $200,000 for a "two-book deal." They would acquire lifetime rights to *The Pathless Path* and fund a second yet-to-be-determined book. Initially excited and flattered by their inquiry, it only took one call with their team for me to know that it was not the right path. They saw my book as one of hundreds in their catalog while I saw it as one of the most important projects of my life. It was easy to walk away.

Through all of this, I kept saying to myself, "*Wow, this is wild.*" It was all so hard to believe. A book I loved writing was making money to fund my life and I was still having fun talking about all the ideas, still connected to my work, and not even close to burning out. It felt so different from my former "good" jobs. *So good.*

Almost three years after publishing the book, I still really enjoy sharing it. It's been interesting to see how other people doing creative work sometimes lose interest in it after they share it with the world. I suspect this happens for a couple of reasons. First, they may be dissatisfied with compromises they made in the work itself to please a broader audience, and second, they burn themselves out in the process of sharing their work by following playbooks rather than doing what feels good. It is easy to default to "best practices," because, well, they work. But in keeping the flame of good work alive, it is vital to think about your approach to all aspects of your work, not just the core thing that matters most.

The most important shift I've made with my work is to start trusting what *already feels good, right now.* When I am in this mode, work feels effortless. It is the opposite of "trying," or what the executive coach Joe Hudson playfully calls, "being at war with yourself."[1] If I tried to be a world-class book marketer, I'd be going against my nature. I would feel tight and eventually, attempt to escape my reality.

The central feature of my relationship with writing is that it is a portal to transcend beyond trying, enabling me to exist fully in the present. This is what good work is all about. It is a place to get lost and completely absorbed in the moment.

10

FIND THE ZEAL

In my consulting jobs, I never felt connected to my work. All of my workplaces were filled with a steady background buzz of activity, and when the inevitable client crisis happened, things ramped up even more. Despite starting every project with bold aims to solve new problems, we would inevitably be sucked into the fire-fighting, political dramas, and client demands that undermine the chance to focus deeply on any kind of meaningful work. Most of us, however, mistook this busyness for progress and productivity.

My friend, author Noah Huisman, has a unique take on this disconnect, pointing out that this busyness could actually be considered "sloth" because "sloth isn't the opposite of industry; it is the opposite of enthusiasm... it is an indifference toward the True, Good, and Beautiful."[1] Understanding this inversion helped me comprehend how I spent ten years in an industry doing an enormous amount of work but feeling as if I created nothing of substance. For most of that time, I had over-looked the fact that I was always being paid to ignore my indifference to the work.

The opposite of sloth is not busyness; instead, it is deep and active engagement with our work. As Noah argues, the word for this is "Zeal." When I slowed down in the first couple of years of self-employment, I consid-ered myself lazy compared to the non-stop pace of consulting. But even though I wasn't "doing" that much or moving fast, I felt this devotional zeal, which I now see as the core energy of good work. When I drop into this state, my life and work feel inevitable. But this mode of being only became accessible to me after I rejected the gospel of constant effort that nudges us to keep working without pause. When I slow down, I'm able to discern between the work I really care about and the "empty calorie" kind of work, like growth hacks, redesigning my website, adopting new productivity tools, and endless networking, which can be so distracting on an entrepreneurial path.

Rejecting the gospel of constant effort is challenging. Even when we enjoy our work, we struggle to believe it could feel effortless and light. The concepts of "effort" and "hard work" are so deeply ingrained in our culture that they can convince us to push past our limits. I've talked with many people who have found work they enjoyed but ended up destroying their relationship with the work by adopting the pace of the world around them, not their own.

Even when people do succeed over the long-term, we tend to ignore subtle descriptions of how people think about their work in favor of the sexier "hustle porn" stories that spread on social media. A recording of Jen-Hsun "Jensen" Huang, the founder of Nvidia, in which he talks about his early struggles, went viral in early 2024. In it, he tells Stanford MBA students, "I wish upon you ample doses of pain and suffering," and addressing the class, he says, "I use the phrase 'pain and suffering'... with great glee."[2] Venture capitalists and hustle bros rejoiced, instantly seeing Huang's remarks as proof that the world is soft and that rewards are justified by personal sacrifice. They shared this message far and wide.

My response to incidents like this is to get curious and research the respective people and viral statements online to see if there is a deeper source of motivation or more telling language behind them. In this case, I found an earlier interview between Huang and Zoom's founder Eric Yuan in which he describes work differently, through the lens of wonder, saying, "If you have an impossible dream, it's incredibly motivating... and it's thrilling to discover the unknown." Referring to his employees, he said that "it's so vital that we create the conditions where they can do their life's work, and they're not making a sacrifice to be here." He said that this only comes from focusing on "what you're doing at the time and not the outcome. The outcome is the result of amazing people doing their life's work, working together to do something the world's never done before."[3] Unsurprisingly, such quotes never go as viral as hustle porn. Yet it sure sounds like Huang is describing good work here, no? In this way, good work often remains a hidden-in-plain-sight secret that too few people become aware of.

Good work *does* involve challenges, but the tendency to glorify pain and suffering as the central element of work blinds us to the reality that most people who are engaged with their work over a long period of time speak of it in glowing, if not holy, terms. They use language like "life's work," "discovering the unknown," and "not making a sacrifice."

Psychologist Dr. Gena Gorlin, who works with many high performers as a coach, points out that the idea that success results from suffering misses the obvious fact that most of the people that actually face extreme suffering "do not achieve great success." The real lesson, she argues, is that "successful people are the ones who manage to find wisdom and perspective from their struggles." They turn their challenges into a positive story. Since we all face challenges in our life, this is a much more useful reframe for thinking about what it takes to develop a positive relationship with work. We aren't succeeding because of our struggles but despite them. Gena argues that many founders and innovators, "often have a 'chip on their shoulder' but it does not explain their greatness; if anything it mitigates their greatness, except insofar as their passion and determination override or compensate for those faults."[4] She argues that remarkable outcomes rarely result from suffering alone. Instead, Gena proposes that, "greatness results from the joyful exercise of agency." She clearly understands good work.

I'm aware of how writing is often described as a "grind," a metaphorical "war" every time you sit down to do it. For me, this resistance only occurs with writing I think I *should* do, like copywriting to promote or sell something. But otherwise I see writing as a beautiful privilege, a far better use of my time than fine-tuning the titles of PowerPoint slides as I did on my previous path. But I'm not saying that writing is easy! There's a subtle distinction between the "grind" associated with writing for external, perhaps hustle-related, purposes and the difficulty of writing for yourself. There is good hard and bad hard. Bad hard is when you are doing things you don't care about. But for me, writing is an example of the good kind of hard. Writing *The Pathless Path* was an enormous challenge. It was hard because I had to learn many things throughout the process. But it was hard *and* something I cared about, and this combination often leads to work that feels good.

This kind of thinking about work is rare. Partly, I suspect, because too few people actually experience deeply connected states in their work, and those who do often lack the language to explain how it feels. I've jokingly argued that many of the people that describe their work with "hustle" language simply haven't read enough poetry or fiction. Until that happens, we should be hesitant to blindly follow other people's formulas for success.

When I started my first job at General Electric (GE), company leaders advised us to follow their paths, seeking out jobs inside the company that were in their words, "impossibly hard." To me, this seemed terrible and I didn't understand why everyone seemed to enthusiastically agree with the advice. But it only bothered me because I didn't care about the success of GE or my unit's attempts to lower the cost by another 1.2%.

Now, with writing, I happily embrace the challenge of getting stuck and feeling frustrated about how to move forward and I don't seem to tire of it. This is because there is no "should" in my relationship to writing. I *care* about it. If writing *required* extreme effort and constant mental contortions, it wouldn't be my good work. In the last six years, I've never come close to feeling burned out and I am still as excited as when I started. I genuinely only write what I want to be writing and stop when I'm losing interest. This allows me to ride the wave of my own interests, staying connected to the work.

When you're disconnected from the work you do, it's a constant struggle because you are moving directly against your own nature. This uncomfortable situation only feels normal if you and everyone else around you have decided this is the only way to live a human adult life. When I worked in consulting, at least once a week someone would say, "I know this is ultimately pointless, but you gotta work, right?"

My answer to this question is "No!" There's another way. Pay attention to what feels right. Follow your genuine interests. Embrace work that gives you a sense of zeal.

This is the path I've taken. I'm still early on my journey, but I look forward to writing and sharing ideas for many more years. If you are able to find a path that feels right, one that is uniquely yours, you can stick around long enough to see interesting things happen.

While I still get wrapped up in "shoulds," I remind myself of the notion that *we want what we actually do.* Instead of thinking about what you "should" be doing, notice what you are already doing. Why not do more of that?

Who knows where it might lead?

11

SEE YOUR WORK AS IT IS

To stay connected to the work that matters to us, we must first have a clear understanding of the stories, expectations, and other baggage we attach to our work. When we strip these away, we are left with simple activities. Then we can pay attention: which ones consistently lead to some level of satisfaction? These are often the core components of our good work. But identifying that work is only the beginning. To stay connected to these activities and let them blossom in the flow of your life, you must master your "inner game."

The concept of the inner game was popularized in the *Inner Game of Tennis,* by author and tennis performance coach W. Timothy Gallwey. In the book, he shares his experience coaching top tennis players. His approach to helping them improve rests on the assumption that everyone has two selves: Self 1, the "Teller," and Self 2, the "Doer." The relationship between the Teller and Doer determines a player's level of improvement.[1] The Teller is the inner voice that says, "You can't do that," or "That was not good enough," or "You should be doing this instead." This voice compares us to others and holds us up to ever higher standards. The Doer, on the other hand, is our natural intuitive self. But it can only take the lead when we quiet the Teller.

This is challenging because many of us are brought up in cultures with scripts that urge us to avoid bad outcomes, be successful, and have our life "figured out." This pressure starts at a young age, as Gallwey points out: "Even before we received praise or blame for our first report card, we were loved or ignored for how well we performed our very first actions."[2] The message that most of us internalize is echoed in the voice of the Teller: "You are a good person and worthy of respect only if you do things successfully." This is exactly the narrative I internalized at the end of high school and by the time I quit my job, I had a hyper-active Teller and an under-developed relationship with my Doer.

Listening to the Teller helps us choose the actions necessary to achieve success based on cultural bench-marks which are future-oriented and externally visible. But these efforts can take us in the opposite direction of good work, which requires us to pay attention to our true interests and desires and rarely comes with a clear path to follow. Instead of focusing on the future, looking for good work means remaining in the present, connected to our own ways of being in the world. It's about moving through life without overthinking, allowing our intuitive self—our Doer—to guide us toward what matters.

For me, the first few years of "just doing" were emotionally intense. I felt insecure about working for myself and being bolder in new domains like writing. *Who was I to think I could be a writer? What business did I have declaring myself self-employed?* I feared the vulnerability that comes with sharing personal thoughts and I lacked people rooting for me. I was in new terrain without a map, filled with insecurity. I was certain I wanted to keep going, but that didn't mean the Teller in my head was quiet. It was a pain in the ass, shouting, "You're a bum!" or "You wasted your career!"

Without a job, I had willingly stepped into the void – the space between a life with a plan and something that was not yet clear. Others didn't understand my worries. My life was set, they thought, why would I willingly put myself through such emotional turmoil? The answer is that despite the discomfort, I was able to exist in the present, which helped me transcend the discomfort. I was embracing the Doer mode and learning to trust my intuition, and I found a surprising amount of satisfaction living in that state.

Eventually I developed a strategy for "talking back" to the Teller's concerns. When my inner voice tried to sabotage me, I would say:

Of course living in the present with things as they are feels like failure. I have no idea what my future looks like and

I'm going against what everyone in the world thinks is safe, smart, and reasonable!

Gallwey refers to this as "seeing your strokes as they are," or more simply, noticing what is happening without judgment. He tells his tennis players, "there are no good or bad strokes." Instead, as he writes, "As soon as a stroke is seen clearly and accepted as it is, a natural and speedy process of change begins." Similarly, on the path of good work, there are no good or bad projects or good or bad days. Everything you do gives you information about yourself. The most important thing is to pay attention. The search for good work can be long and confusing and any story you whip up in your head about what you "should" be doing or how you are failing will lengthen that journey. If I am writing and struggling to make progress, I notice that. I don't see it as proof of being a "struggling writer," or even "embracing the grind," I'm simply writing. If I am working on a project and feel my body contract, that's vital information. Something is off and I need to be skeptical of the voice that tells me to ignore it and to keep going. I try to embrace this practice fully, treating my days and projects with lightness, rejecting judgment. None of my work is the right or wrong thing to be doing. Each moment is simply a chance to pay attention and learn.[3]

Gallwey found that when tennis players perceive their weaknesses as "problems," they get stuck in the belief that improving requires fixing those problems. But in this frame, the players implicitly see themselves as broken. If I saw my lack of interest in marketing and book launches as a problem, I might have spent years reinventing myself in that vein. But the only result would have been burning out and becoming disconnected from what matters.

If you look for problems, you will find them. Philosopher Andrew Taggart calls this tendency "the problematization of the world."[4] As he argues, "The world writ large is not a problem to be solved." Despite this, we diagnose endless problems in our lives and the world at large and are presented with books, ideas, playbooks, influencers, and products that are happy to offer solutions. We become convinced that once we solve all of our problems, all will be okay. Taggart argues that there are two basic ways to solve a problem in this frame: "Get rid of it" or "Give it an upgrade." For example, with regard to work, "Get rid of it" might mean embracing the idea that you can "escape" work by retiring early and living on a beach. In the corporate world, I was constantly seduced by "Give it an upgrade" advice, convinced that if I could just embrace things like job crafting or fine-tuning my personal values, I'd land a perfect job that would solve all of life's problems once and for all.

But what if your life contains no problems to solve? What if you are already good enough? How would this change how you approach your path? In terms of work, you likely already know what matters to you and what kind of work that you'd like to do more of. Just pay attention to that. If it's writing, you don't need bootcamps, courses, software, a certain kind of pen, or anything else. You just need to sit down and write. If you struggle, just notice what is coming up. Don't tell yourself you *should* be better at this. Ask yourself questions instead. Get curious about it. Try again the next day. Don't take it so seriously.

If you approach the search for good work as a problem to be solved, you will create an endless string of more distracting problems. I used to be a problem-solver extraordinaire, desperate to "solve" the problem of not being happy at work. But I never came close to cracking the code because I didn't spend a single second slowing down and trying to figure out what I really wanted. Ultimately, I realized I was looking at life through a lens that was far too narrow. I love Taggart's alternative to a problem-based reality: "learn to ask wide-ranging, fundamental questions about life, and seek answers that give rise to further questions instead of blindly seeking a single answer." Essentially, he is saying, "Be present; contemplate."

But this is hard to do and even harder to explain to others:

"Why aren't you trying to find a better job?"

"Oh, I'm just leaning into the flow of the universe and seeing where I end up."

"Um..."

You might think I want everyone to quit their jobs. I

don't. I just want to convince you that a better relationship to work is possible. And once you know this kind of path exists, the right way to find it is to be open to it, to ask lots of questions, and to assume, despite your doubts, that you are already on the right path.

But trusting yourself is hard. We crave approval or permission, wanting to know we are on the "right" path. But following your own path inevitably makes you feel as if you are doing something wrong. This is an opportunity to connect with our inner Doer, something we all have access to. Gallwey explains that "there is a natural learning process which operates within everyone – if it is allowed to. This process is waiting to be discovered by all those who do not know of its existence..." This book is about *discovering* this process for work and cultivating trust in what it might tell you.

This way of being goes against all of our culturally conditioned instincts. When we lack an "inner game," we default to playing the "outer game," which is more accepted in our culture. In the "outer game," we seek to bend the world to our will. If we don't get what we desire, we double down on our efforts. I played this game for years. Rather than slowing down to explore my inner world, I adopted any "solution" that offered an easier path forward. My current path is a useful corrective as it forces me to live on the frontier of my own comfort. On a pathless path you *must* develop an inner game. Just like Gallwey urged his players to "see their strokes as they are," you must:

See your experiments as they are.
See your work as it is.
See your days as they are.

Staying present in this way was quite hard for me in the conventional career world, where the scorecard of outer game metrics was seemingly all anyone cared about. Because my outer game achievements were impressive, having a pathetically weak inner game was overlooked. I ignored my discontent, however, because my inner Teller kept saying, "You should appreciate what you have." This self-gaslighting was the same mistake Gallwey's students made. I was telling myself how I *should* feel rather than noticing what I was actually experiencing. When I dropped the *should*, I was able to see clearly that I didn't like what I was doing.

The paycheck world doesn't give a damn if you have an inner game that allows you to discover work that matters to you. You can go inward on your own, but it's certainly not required. I've met people that *can* find work that matters to them in a conventional setting. I couldn't. But shifting my perspective, trusting myself, and noticing what was happening rather than trying to solve a series of never ending "problems" has led to every interesting turn my life has taken since.

People underestimate how well things might work out if you don't have a plan. This is because they don't have much practice sitting in the present and noticing the abundance of wisdom and clues that surround us. If you can sit with the inherent discomfort and uncertainty of not moving forward in a world that doesn't stop, opportunities tend to magically emerge.

Don't deny this magic.

PART FOUR
COMMIT TO
GOOD WORK

"You can measure your worth by your dedication to your path, not by your successes or failures."[1]

— ELIZABETH GILBERT

"Often, I've wished that I could've had quicker success, greater financial security, more respect, et cetera, as a writer. For nearly twelve years now since leaving the law, I have often felt ashamed for wanting to be a writer and doubtful of my talents. What helped in these moments was to consider what was important, rather than the urgent feelings of embarrassment and helplessness. What was important is still important now: to learn to write better in order to better complete the vision one holds in one's head and to enjoy the writing, because the work has to be the best part."[2]

— MIN JIN LEE

12

LEAVE MONEY ON THE TABLE

As I've described my transformation from a consultant with a good job to a writer with good work, you've probably been thinking: what about money? *Is this guy some rich multi-millionaire? Trust fund? How the hell am I supposed to follow this path? I have a mortgage and daycare and bills to pay!*

The truth is that I worry about money all the time. However, by learning to co-exist with my fear and discomfort, I can decide to worry more about other things. But this transformation has not been easy. When I quit my job, I was in a good position: single, no debt, and a year's worth of living expenses in savings. But these advantages could not protect me from the tsunami of emotions that hit immediately after I quit my job: *Good god, what have I done? I might go broke.*

The feelings of scarcity shocked me. Because I worried about money much less than the people around me, I was convinced I was immune. But by quitting, I realized that my feelings of safety while employed had always been an illusion. I "left money on the table" many times in my career, choosing to take a pay cut to join McKinsey & Company and missing out on bonuses upon taking new jobs. Despite these choices, I was protected by the comforts of continuous employment. In my last job, I even repaid a $24,000 signing bonus when leaving, not having worked the full three years required to keep it. I remember the pain I felt while slowly writing the check on my living room table. I was signing away a third of my savings, and I was about to by fully responsible for making money on my own.

Self-employment was a jarring wakeup call. I felt free with $50,000 in savings before quitting, but as soon as I saw that amount start to shrink, I felt the world closing in around me. Halfway through the first year, after I had started to make some money, someone suggested a new way of thinking about money that helped. They said, "why not consider the savings a gift from your former self?" *Hmm. That was interesting.* I could be grateful to "achiever Paul" for making this money and giving me the chance to reinvent myself. I loved the idea and I'm not sure why it worked, but in that moment, I gave myself permission to enjoy my life much more. While employed, my savings was for retirement, something I wasn't supposed to enjoy until I was 65 years old. But now I asked myself, "*Why wait?!*"

This new perspective gave me permission to live differently and since I've been self-employed, I've prioritized flexibility, autonomy, and working less over trying to earn more money. Having slack in my schedule and knowing I don't have to "show up" to work has given me unexpected relief and a sense of comfort. When I first quit my job, I was surprised to discover this possibility, something which was never possible while employed. With lingering issues since a health crisis in 2012, including multiple months-long stretches of fatigue, I've benefited from an unexpected "feature" of this path: being able to ramp down my work within a couple of days in order to focus on my health.

Writing about this realization in my first year of self-employment, I reflected that I could "take time to recharge, spend time with family or focus on projects that I'm excited by to make the journey a lot more sustainable." I shared my intention to exercise this freedom: "My goal for this summer is to spend 50 days with my grandmother and family at the family lake house."[1] That summer was a success and I'll always remember us sitting around, talking, playing cards, and generally just enjoying each other's company. My grandmother was one of my biggest supporters and I'm so grateful for the quality time I had with her before she passed.

"But Paul, how does it really feel to leave money on the table?" you still ask.

Most of the time? I feel like a fool.

That summer I spent with my grandmother also included visits with my parents, aunts, uncles, and cousins. Not only are all of their lives built around full-time employment, but most of them are crushing it *and* they enjoy it. They struggled to understand what I was doing.

Was I taking a break?

Did I have a plan?

Shouldn't I be working on something?

How long did I intend to stay in Taiwan?

Wasn't I worried about making money?

Each question triggered my insecurity. What *was* I doing? I had a strong sense that I wanted to stay on my path, but I was still months away from becoming aware of my connection to writing. If I had only known what I'd learn in Taiwan and then Bali and in the years since, I might have been less fragile. This is a constant challenge on this path, because those who point out the "risks" of this path are 100% correct. It's just that they can't "see" the benefits, like aliveness, curiosity, and peace of mind.

A conversation with the organizational psychologist and coach Tim Malnick helped give me the language for these contrasting perspectives. In his words, I was embracing the "life path" rather than "money path." To him, those on the "money path" see money as the answer to life's problems and that, "one day, when I sort this out, I'll get to do what I want." Suffer now for a future payoff. In contrast, on the "life path" you can "do what you love, and the more you follow it, the more you will have your needs met with and without money."[2] And the key here is that on the life path, your needs are met with *and without* money, which is what I've experienced. I've left tons of money on the table, but I've been compensated generously with space to think and grow as a person, time with Angie and Michelle, new friends who are willing to spend time with me, and an overall psychological richness that I would never give up. Many of the costs of this path, like uncertainty, have become a small price to pay for the sense of abundance and expanded sense of agency I feel on a day-to-day basis.

Despite barely breaking even in my first four years of self-employment, my days were delightful and that became a reward in itself. The longer I went like that, the better I felt about my life. Sure, I stopped saving for the future, something others saw as a risk, but in return, I got a life I loved. This helped break the connection in my head between living a good life and consistently earning more money. Trading money for time and enjoyment was worth it, and I became convinced to keep making such trade-offs.

However, these trade-offs do have real costs. On

paper, I have undoubtedly sacrificed earnings, and when you see the numbers, it may be hard for you to want to make similar choices. Based on a comparison of the actual earnings I've made over the past 7+ years (including an estimate of this year's earnings) with a very conservative estimate of what I would have earned if I had simply kept going on my consulting path, which would you choose, Path #1 or Path #2?

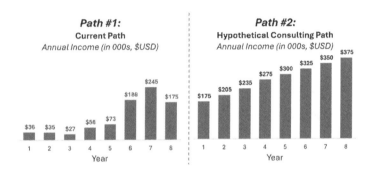

Path #1:
Current Path
Annual Income (in 000s, $USD)

Path #2:
Hypothetical Consulting Path
Annual Income (in 000s, $USD)

It seems pretty crazy to turn down Path #2, right?

But this is the fundamental problem of making life decisions on a spreadsheet. It overlooks the fact that on Path #1, my actual life, I've spent 98% of my time on my terms and through that, I have built a life where I feel incredibly content and fulfilled. It also includes publishing my first book, which is something that feels like it would have been impossible on Path #2. In fact, it's hard to make any sort of reasonable comparison between the two paths because my worldview and fundamental enthusiasm for life are so radically differ- ent. If you had presented these numbers to me in 2017, I think I would have still made the same choice to walk away, but it would have been harder.

Control over my time is the reason it's so easy for me to leave money on the table. Every time I make a decision not to pursue an opportunity, it doesn't feel like losing money, it feels like I'm reaffirming my commitment to this path. When I worked full-time, the obvious approach to life was to prioritize money above other goals. Why? Because you usually can't negotiate for more time. Maybe you can work four days a week or get another week of vacation, but you are expected to be devoting a majority of your attention to your job. In this reality, it makes sense to try to earn as much as possible each year.

I've had practice making these decisions, but this doesn't mean it is easy. Right before committing to writing my first book, with millions of people working remotely due to the pandemic, there was unprecedented demand for online courses and virtual learning experiences. I was perfectly positioned. My StrategyU consulting skills course targeted high-wage knowledge workers – the exact people who now found themselves working remotely and with generous company learning stipends to spend. While I did see a boost in demand for my self-paced course, there was a very clear opportunity to create a "high-ticket" live version where I'd work directly with students. I could easily charge $2,000 or more per person. Some friends were making nearly half a million dollars from a single course. The pull was strong. I could see the future six-figure sums on my screen.

For the previous two years, my life had been simple. Living on less than $2,000 a month, covered by the passive income from my course, I focused on writing and following my curiosity. I never sought additional paid work, so my commitment remained untested. Now, there was a fork in the road. I could talk myself into doing the live course. Yet I found myself asking, "Then what? What would I do with all that money?" It was obvious. I would "buy time" to write.

The StrategyU work, while still "good enough" work, and far better than the consulting projects I had moved away from, would still require me to grind. Writing a book, in comparison, felt easier even though I didn't have any experience. I had no idea how to write a book but I was excited by the prospect of figuring it out. So I chose the book, and as I started writing it in Mexico, I could feel the imaginary future payoff instantly dissolve. But I didn't care. Writing was my good work and I needed to see where it took me.

However, in making this decision, I did not instantly become immune to distractions. This is one of the challenges of being self-employed: you can literally work on anything you want at any time. While writing the book, in 2021, I got swept up in the crypto mania around NFTs for a few weeks. One night, Angie and I were at an Airbnb in Fuli, Taiwan. As Angie went to bed and turned the lights off, I pulled out my laptop, dimming the screen to a faint glow in the dark room. I opened the Discord channel I had recently joined to stay up to date on the latest NFT "drops." It was just past midnight, but I still had an hour to go until I could "mint" the digital image from the collection I'd been following. I looked over to Angie, deep in sleep, and felt silly. I started to question myself, "What the hell am I doing?" I didn't care about crypto, and for years I had been writing about the joy of doing things you care about rather than chasing money. I closed my laptop and never looked at any sort of crypto project again until my book was published six months later.

Opportunities like this can be even more seductive if you are working on something that doesn't earn money. For me, it has been disorienting to spend most of my time writing without any promise of monetary rewards after a decade of getting paid for every single hour I worked. For the three years prior to writing *The Pathless Path*, I spent thousands of hours writing and made less than $2,000 from those efforts. But I realized that if I prioritized making money from writing, I would have to write things that I didn't care about and in doing so, I'd be sucked into the pressures that come with the identity of *being* a "writer." Instead, I thought about my creative work like a business might think about investing in research & development for a product that takes years to come to market. But instead of investing money, I was investing time and energy. And like a business, I was comfortable with the idea that it might not pay off financially. But the arbitrage was always having the time of my life along the way.

Leaving money on the table does not mean *never* making money. In fact, it might mean making *more money later.* I spent years writing about work before publishing my first book, but now it might generate income for the rest of my life. How much you leave on the table will depend on the trade-offs unique to your good work and your personal risk tolerance. If you fully commit to good work, at some point you will inevitably feel as if you are underachieving or under-earning. However, maximizing income at all costs can be a risky strategy because you are optimizing for what the market is telling you to do, not what you can actually sustain.

Most people eventually come to this realization, especially when they care about their relationship to the work and how it makes them feel. For instance, in a reflective video, YouTuber Ali Abdaal talked about the tension he feels between optimizing for income on his channel and his own continued interest in the work. He realized that if "money were no object," he would still make videos, but he would only make them when he was "called to do it." But he reflected, "What is stopping me from doing this?" It was simple, he realized: "money." He would have to "leave money on the table." But if he wanted to build a life around enjoying his work and a path that felt "good" and "authentic," he knew this was the only way forward. He reflected on what committing to making only things that he cared about would mean for his bottom line: "That probably means I'll have a smaller business than other people and...will sell less books than other people might, but that's okay."[3]

This is the truth. When you commit to work that matters to you and lean into that life, it will feel like you are lighting current and future opportunities on fire. During Michelle's first year of life, I made more money than ever from my writing, But this income resulted from the book, something I had written before her birth. I took the surprising increase in earnings to give myself permission to fully embrace an extended "paternity leave." I didn't work much that entire year and knew it would likely lead to a dip in future income. Indeed, as I write this, sales of my first book are about 60% lower than last year and my total income will likely be down about 40%. Does this make me nervous? Of course! But do I wish I had done anything different? Hell, no! The whole reason for leaving the default path was to step into life and spend more time with my kids when I eventually had them.

In Abdaal's video, he cites an email he received from an entrepreneur, April Perry, that helped him find comfort with leaving money on the table. Perry wrote, "People always talk about leaving money on the table like it's a terrible thing. Why don't you sell another digital product? Why don't you do a mastermind? Why don't you sell physical products? But no one ever speaks of the mental and emotional costs associated with managing all of that." She added that we need to reframe this mindset: "Why are you leaving peace of mind on the table? Why are you leaving family time on the table?... Can you laugh and sing and truly relax with loved ones?" Perry has come to see that "if I have my family's financial needs covered, the first thing I'll leave on the table is money."

Perry's words made me realize that I've internalized a similar trade-off. Leaving money on the table is *easy* for me because I am no longer willing to leave soul or peace of mind on the table. The path of good work is defined by unconventional trade-offs. Think about what you won't leave on the table. Soul? Your relationships? Time freedom? Your health? That book you want to write? Time with your kids in the "magic window"?

I've read many books about people's regrets at the end of their lives or after "making it" and they almost all say the same thing: "I wish I hadn't worked so much," or "I should have done more of what mattered." I've tried to inject the spirit of these sentiments into my own life by regularly asking myself, "What if I skip aiming at other people's idea of what I should be doing?" The surprising result is that I feel more successful on my new path, even at times when I have been making 80% less than my previous path. This works because the journey is the reward itself. For me, it is far more enjoyable and feels sustainable. *I feel good, right now.* There is nowhere to go and nothing to be fixed. By going against the grain and slowing down, I'm able to craft my life around activities I definitely want to keep doing. I can take a long term view toward a life that I am committed to, without the desire to escape.

Leaving money on the table has enabled me to find something far more valuable: the satisfaction of a life designed around work that matters to me. This doesn't mean I'm opposed to making a lot more money (please share the book far and wide to help make that happen!). Rather it's about prioritizing what can't be bought, a life built around good work, one that I'm excited to keep living.

13
RECLAIM YOUR AMBITION

Taipei, September 2021.

I'm walking around the streets of Taipei after getting a coffee at 7-11, one of the only places you can get coffee before 10am. As a nearby light turns green, I hear a cacophony of scooters revving their engines as if they are drag-racing.

I'm ten months into writing my first book. The week before, I was in the south of Taiwan and an impromptu scooter ride helped me understand what the book was all about. Despite lots of work remaining, I know I can complete the book.

I think, "*Wow, I am going to pull this off.*"

At the same time, I'm nervous. This is the boldest thing I've done with my writing. *What happens next?*

Three years prior, also in Taipei, I had committed myself to following this path and to my connection with writing, no matter where it took me. It was a fun journey.

I had fallen in love, gotten married, and traveled the world. I had come to know myself deeply for the first time in my life.

But also, during those three years, I had been hiding. I needed to make sense of blowing up my life, and writing had served as a consistent refuge.

The buzz of the scooters fades as I take a turn down a tiny alley, an instant escape from the noise of the city. I start thinking about the book.

Publishing it means I'll be putting everything I think out into the world. There is no hiding anymore. Everyone I know can read it and it will exist, out there in the world, forever.

I return to the coliving hostel, grab my microphone and laptop, and walk down to the coworking office. I open my computer and get set up to record a podcast.

Today, I'm talking with my friend Kris, someone I've been begging to do a podcast interview for months, his first. He finally agreed.

As soon as we start, I'm lost in the conversation. I want to know everything. *What's it like not having a "regular" job as a parent? How did it feel to leave a lucrative career like trading behind? How do you apply probabilistic thinking to life decisions?* Like me, he's battling the uncertainty of leaving behind a path that made sense and searching for something else. I love talking to people like this. They are hungry, open and curious. They also make me feel a little less crazy.

The conversation ends, "Alright. Recording is off. That was fun. Thanks for finally doing that!"

He agrees, and we keep chatting.

He praises my writing again and thanks me for everything I've done. I feel shy. He's giving me too much credit.

"You're a hyper-curious person," I tell him. "You would figure this stuff out on your own even without people like me."

"Whatever you say. what you're doing is great, I hope you keep doing it," he replies.

I admit, "I am having so much fun on this path, but sometimes I do feel reckless."

Then, staring at his laptop screen, he casually leans back in his chair and says something that shocks me, "Forget all that, what you're doing is bold. You're one of the most ambitious people I've met."

"Me? Ambitious? Nah," I think.

He just sits there.

Oh wait, he's serious.

I start generating proof that he's wrong in my head but realize I'm fighting a war against myself, for no reason.

I accept the compliment.

For days afterward, I can't stop thinking about his comment.

Kris is one of the sharpest people I know. What does he see that I can't?

As I wander around the streets and alleys of Taipei, the question comes with me, "Am I ambitious?"

His comment sat with me for the next year. Through a move back to the U.S. and the launch of my book, I kept thinking about what Kris said: *Ambitious. Why am I so resistant to this word? Am I actually ambitious? If so, what does that mean?*

Earlier, I had always equated ambition with the default path of success. The path I left behind. There the definition of ambition was simple: an ambitious person aims at money, status, and an impressive career path.

But slowly, I started to realize that my journey after quitting my job has reflected another kind of ambition. It wouldn't land me on the cover of *Fortune*, but it has led me somewhere far better: to a life where I feel I can thrive.

After moving to the U.S., I felt the pressure of higher living costs, which motivated me to become a little more pragmatic about making money. So I put myself, and my writing, out into the world. Slowly, and on my terms, I actively promoted my book. I asked people if I could go on their podcasts. I gifted hundreds of copies of my book. I shared updates about my sales. I playfully poked fun at the traditional publishing world after rejecting their offer.

And what I felt surprised me.

Nothing. I was fine.

For years, I had been convinced I was on a cliff's edge. If I pushed myself too hard, I'd ruin everything and fall off the cliff. But this feeling was not related to any real, external situation – it was all in my body. It was fear. I was afraid of ending up back where I started: dissatisfied, lost, and stuck in a job I wanted to escape. With each step I took, however, I realized I was far from that metaphorical edge. I was on firm ground.

Through committing to good work in Taiwan and Bali, and following the energy that the work gave me, I had found my place. I found a path where I could fully show up as myself. There was no risk of losing myself because I was doing everything from a firm foundation of trust. Not only in myself, but in the world.

Through good work, I slowly reclaimed my own inner ambition and steered it back toward my own aims. But despite Kris telling me I was ambitious, and many other friends saying similar things, I couldn't quite admit it to myself.

One day, about a year after launching my book, I looked at myself in the mirror and said, "*I am ambitious.*" My voice faded as I said the word. I still couldn't fully say it. Some part of me was still afraid that I was casting a spell that might instantly transform me into a hustle bro, ready to abandon my family in pursuit of shareholder value.

So I said it again, "I am ambitious."

And I realized: *I was okay.*

I've come to understand that one of the most ambitious things we can do, following our own true path, does not *feel* like we might expect ambition to feel. It does not come with pain, or contraction, or endless suffering. Instead, it feels light. It feels natural, as if everything you are meant to be doing is obvious. And all you need to do to "be ambitious" is simply to follow this feeling and stay connected to it.

Our culture will attempt to steal your inner ambition and convince you to use it to do what organizations, your parents, or your manager might want. But this is not your ambition. Your ambition desires more than a job title, a salary, or a brand-name company. It is a fire that burns inside of you—not for a bigger paycheck, but for a bigger life.

Your mission is to make sure that this flame never dies.

There were always clues pointing me away from my "good" jobs and toward good work. Jumping from engineering to operations to finance to consulting to human resources, I never gave up hope that there was a place for me. Every time someone told me that I should stop switching jobs, I became more determined. Something deep inside of me compelled me to keep searching.

For what? I was never quite sure, but it scares me to think that I might have given up. In my final full-time job, I felt doomed. Before I started, I told myself I'd stick around for at least five years. I would prove I was not a job-hopper after all. Eighteen months in, I knew I wouldn't make it. When I quit, it wasn't an exciting step. It felt like giving up. But now I know it was just the start of reclaiming my inner ambition, snatching it back from the achievement culture in which I had been drowning.

I wrote this book for my former self. I wish I had stumbled upon ideas like this earlier. So that I could have recognized that behind my desire to escape work was a deeper desire to build a life around work that mattered.

Ten years ago, I was deep in the path of a default path achiever, spending my time on things I didn't care about. Now, I've reinvented myself in ways that I never imagined possible. Since discovering my good work, my life is oriented toward things I genuinely care about. I don't know how much longer I can keep this going, but it doesn't matter. I'm having a ton of fun, right now, and the past seven years working for myself have been the most nourishing of my life.

As I approach the end of this second book, I'm sitting here once again, smiling like a fool, deeply connected to my work, right where I am meant to be. I don't know how I pulled this off again, but I did. *Wow*.

It's a beautiful thing and I feel like the luckiest man in the world.

I want this for you, too. Really. I want to see you bring the full force of your inner ambition into the world.

A CALL TO ACTION

I believe that searching for, finding, and embracing good work is one of the most noble quests of our age.

My goal with this book is to convince you that finding good work is *possible* and that searching for it is worth it.

My path to good work took years and involved many challenges along the way. In this book I've shared the most honest account of what I experienced, hoping to make your journey a little easier.

Wherever your path may lead, I hope you'll accept this challenge:

Embark on the search for good work.
It's the most ambitious thing you can do.

FINAL REFLECTIONS

In order to help you on your path to finding and committing to good work, I wanted to leave you with thirteen thoughts from this book.

These are not only principles I was able to recommit to through writing, I genuinely think they can help you build a life around work that matters.

#1 Follow your interests. Ask yourself: when was the last time you felt like you were fully alive and connected to work of any kind? Many people have skills that help them make money, but if you focus primarily on those skills, you might overlook your deepest curiosities and interests. What did you do as a child that you loved? Which activities cause you to lose track of time when you do them? Are you already doing something that you might not be taking seriously? I was writing for years until I saw it as work worth doing. What might you be missing that's right in front of you?

#2 Slow down to move forward: Too few people take intentional breaks from work. But when they do, they often encounter clues that help them understand what they want out of work and life. An intentional break or a structured sabbatical can provide a temporary reprieve from the pressures of the modern world and space to experiment. You can sample the uncertainty of an unconventional path and see if you want to keep going. As people slow down, they rediscover forgotten hobbies and start creative projects. Almost everyone who's taken an intentional break from work has told me they wish they took one sooner. It might be the only "hack" I fully endorse.

#3 Appreciate the non-monetary benefits of good work. Once you've discovered your good work, resist the urge to make money from it immediately. This can be challenging, especially if you are used to optimizing your skills and work for profit. It is tempting to seek quick financial gains at the start of your search for good work as proof that you are on to something. Be patient. Notice the non-monetary benefits your good work gives you like peace of mind, a sense of fulfillment, and joy. Making money from your good work is great, just make sure you don't undermine the things that make it so special.

#4 Question the default path and work scripts. Many people grow up with inherited scripts about work that shape their beliefs and actions. These scripts often emphasize suffering, financial success, and career advancement as central to a good life. Be open to questioning these scripts. Are they still serving you? Reflect on the simple but hard question of "What is work?" Does your overall story make sense given the opportunities you have in the world? How can you rewrite your own story of work such that it aligns with your own inner ambition?

#5 Embrace the long, slow, stupid, fun way. Look for ways to slow down to make it easier for you to stay "in the game." If you can find a path where you start to feel confident about continuing to do something over a long period of time, you will have no competition. The biggest challenge when you go slower is dealing with feeling "stupid," or not doing your "best." Going slower allows you to stay on your path longer. And when you find a path you can stay on, one that is uniquely yours? It will be more fun than you expect.

#6 Bring your insecurities along with you. The path of good work is not about escaping insecurities — it is about facing them head on. Embracing the messy emotions of an uncertain path, like fear and uncertainty, can transform them from painful obstacles into manageable companions on our journey. This unlocks many "hidden" benefits of such a path: a sense of agency, a feeling of satisfaction from doing work you care about, creative energy, alignment between work and personal values, a renewable source of motivation, time freedom and flexibility, and an overall sense of purpose. While these may not gain you instant approval like an impressive job might, they outweigh the inherent uncertainties of an unconventional path. By embracing rather than avoiding emotions, you discover that your previous coping strategies were often counterproductive. Ask yourself: *If you are going to feel uncertain and afraid anyway, why not go after your true ambitions?*

#7 **Find a positive "edge."** Good work can be compatible with the "edge" that some people develop from a sense of lack, but in my experience, this eventually leads to burnout. This is because good work does not come with the comforting guardrails of a stable income and employment that traditional work offers. If you are trying to run from both your own insecurities and the inherent uncertainty of your path, you will end up running in circles. It's easier over the long-term to slow down and pay attention to the natural energy that your connection with good work provides, and once you trust the connection, you can start to use it as renewable energy to pull you forward on your path and in life.

#8 **Don't mistake a good job for good work.** Good jobs are abundant and offer us comfort and a sense of achievement. But don't "should" yourself into staying in one of these positions when your heart and soul yearn for more. Do an inventory of what you are sacrificing to maintain this good job existence. Is it worth it? If so, great. If not, what would you sacrifice to find your good work? Remember, work isn't only employment. It can be an activity that "pays" you in rewards beyond money. Your "I'll do it one day" dreams will eventually expire. Don't risk that. Consider that by leaving a situation that looks great on paper, you might actually find another that's far better.

#9 Solve the puzzle of good work. The puzzle of good work is always in flux and requires constant tinkering, reflection, and patience. Once you identify the core activities of your good work, the journey is just beginning. Look for ways to experiment with how and when you work. Think beyond the workday or workweek toward "work months" "work years" and even "work decades." Become aware of supporting activities that may fuel your curiosity, passion, and creativity, but remember not to mistake them for your good work itself. Mastering this puzzle also requires discipline. Try to create "good enough" work that can help fund your journey without draining your energy and, if it helps you keep your journey alive, don't avoid "bad" work completely. Solving the puzzle is about always trying to find your way back to your good work no matter how long you've been disconnected.

#10 Don't "should" yourself. Become skeptical of your inner "Teller" and develop a stronger relationship with your inner "Doer." This will strengthen your intuition about following the work that feels right. Trusting your intuition is all about *seeing your work as it is.* If you enjoy something, pay attention, that's important. But similarly, if you are grinding your way through something, *that's important to recognize too.* Don't "should" yourself into doing work that drains you. The inner game of good work is not about seeking others' approval, but instead sharpening your own connection to a certain kind of work. There are no good or bad days when you're searching for good work – everything is an opportunity to learn.

#11 Look for unconventional trade-offs. If you aren't "leaving money on the table," you are likely missing trade-offs that may not only improve your life, but also enable you to make a longer-term commitment to good work. First, identify the values that are important to you. Creative expression? Freedom? Peace of mind? Family? If you don't know what you truly value, you will be pulled toward the defaults of "more" and "bigger" which shape our current work reality. It can be useful to look at people you admire. What interesting trade-offs are they making? Remember, you can always make more money, but you can't ever get back time. Embrace the idea that "leaving money on the table" isn't losing – it's simply a way of reaffirming your commitment to your life. And who knows, maybe you'll end up making more money along the way too.

#12 Have faith in good work. Finding and committing to good work requires patience, persistence, and faith. It's a personal journey that everyone must go through in their own way. Even once you find your good work, you may struggle to stay connected to it. This is normal. But each time you reconnect with your good work, you'll gain more confidence to keep going. Remember, most people quit. But don't quit. The search for your good work can be long and confusing, but for many, it feels impossible to abandon once they've found it. Have faith that by staying connected to work that matters to you, interesting and unexpected things will happen over time.

#13 Reclaim your inner ambition. At some point, a fire burning inside of you steered you in a certain direction in life. Perhaps you loved the initial path you embarked on, much like I enjoyed consulting in my first couple of years. If that fire has become a small flame, vow to yourself: I will not let this flame die. Embrace this urgent mission. Embark on the search for good work. It might be a way to reclaim your own inner ambition, the deepest expression of who you really want to be in the world.

QUOTES THAT INSPIRED
THIS BOOK

During the writing of this book, I kept a file of quotes that inspired me. Some of them made them into the text and others are here, sorted by topic.

ON PAYING ATTENTION

"Vocation does not come from willfulness. It comes from listening. I must listen to my life and try to understand what it is truly about — quite apart from what I would like it to be about — or my life will never represent anything real in the world, no matter how earnest my intentions"[1]

— PARKER PALMER

ON STAYING CONNECTED TO YOUR WORK

"The man who works recognizes his own product in the World that has actually been transformed by his work: he recognizes himself in it, he sees in it his own human reality, in it he discovers and reveals to others the objective reality of his humanity, of the originally abstract and purely subjective idea he has of himself."[2]

— ALEXANDRE KOJÈVE

"A third way of attaining union lies in creative activity, be it that of the artist, or of the artisan. In any kind of creative work, the creating person unites himself with his material, which represents the world outside of himself. Whether a carpenter makes a table, or a goldsmith a piece of jewelry, whether the peasant grows his corn or the painter paints a picture, in all types of creative work the worker and his object become one, man unites himself with the world in the process of creation. This, however, holds true only for productive work, for work in which I plan, produce, see the result of my work. In the modern work process of a clerk, the worker on the endless belt, little is left of this uniting quality of work. The worker becomes an appendix to the machine or to the bureaucratic organization. He has ceased to be he—hence no union takes place beyond that of conformity."[3]

— ERICH FROMM

ON "NOT WORKING"

"But I don't like working. I do the absolute minimum that is necessary to reach a decision. There are many people who love working. They amass an inordinate amount of information, much more than is necessary to reach a conclusion. And they become attached to certain investments because they know them intimately. I am different. I concentrate on the essentials. When I have to, I work furiously because I am furious that I have to work. When I don't have to, I don't work."[4]

— GEORGE SOROS

ON DOING WORK YOU LOVE

"The important thing is how much you can come to understand, which of your abilities you can develop, how far you can grow. The priorities of our culture, however, are completely different.

The culture decrees that you should do what you are good at rather than what you most like to do; that what you produce rather than what you get out of what you produce is what counts; that your ability, reflected in achievements, is what matters. Given cultural expectations, it is all too easy to equate personal and professional worth. Once the two are disentangled, work becomes less symbolic and therefore less problematic."[5]

— VIRGINIA VALIAN

"It's tragic to see men and women wasting their lives in work that they hate or do badly. It's never too late to find out that you're doing something you don't like, and are not very good at. Then you've got to take hold of yourself and decide what you would like to be doing most and then do it for the rest of your life."[6]

— DAVID OGILVY

"Don't lose faith. I'm convinced that the only thing that kept me going was that I loved what I did. You've got to find what you love. And that is as true for your work as it is for your lovers. Your work is going to fill a large part of your life, and the only way to be truly satisfied is to do what you believe is great work. And the only way to do great work is to love what you do. If you haven't found it yet, keep looking. Don't settle. As with all matters of the heart, you'll know when you find it. And, like any great relationship, it just gets better and better as the years roll on. So keep looking until you find it. Don't settle."[7]

— STEVE JOBS

ON FINDING YOUR OWN PACE

"Once I go into that contrived place where I'm efforting something too much, it's going to be bad."[8]

— JASON FRIED

"In an age of speed, I began to think, nothing could be more invigorating than going slow. In an age of distraction, nothing can feel more luxurious than paying attention. And in an age of constant movement, nothing is more urgent than sitting still."[9]

— PICO IYER

"The really hard thing about writing is how much patience you need to have. I mean, you can will things, but whenever I've tried to do that, the poem just goes to hell. Becomes a contrivance. An arrangement made with a mind instead of a discovery. If you want a discovery that will surprise you, too, you just have to wait... What's needed is not diligence or intelligence. What's needed is an intervention of something outside yourself, better than yourself, but with access to yourself... The gift I have is stubbornness. And patience."[10]

— LOUISE GLÜCK

"There is almost no life a human being can construct for themselves where they are not wrestling with something difficult, something that takes a modicum of work. The only possibility seems to be the ability of human beings to choose good work. At its simplest, good work, is work that makes sense, and that grants sense and meaning to the one who is doing it and to those affected by it."[11]

— DAVID WHYTE

ON WORK AS A BROADER CONNECTION TO LIFE

"There is work that is isolating, harsh, destructive, specialized or trivialized into meaninglessness. And there is work that is restorative, convivial, dignified and dignifying, and pleasing. Good work is not just the maintenance of connections—as one is now said to work "for a living" or "to support a family"—but the enactment of connections. It is living, and a way of living; it is not support for a family in the sense of an exterior brace or prop, but is one of the forms and acts of love."[12]

— WENDELL BERRY

"Do whatever brings you to life, then. Follow your own fascinations, obsessions, and compulsions. Trust them. Create whatever causes a revolution in your heart."[13]

— ELIZABETH GILBERT

"For there a perennial nobleness, and even sacredness, in Work. Were he never so benighted, forgetful of his high calling, there is always hope in a man that actually and earnestly works: in Idleness alone is there perpetual despair."[14]

— THOMAS CARLYLE

ON CARING & COMMITTING TO YOUR WORK

"Our society frowns on people who set out to do really good work. You're not supposed to; luck is supposed to descend on you and you do great things by chance. Well, that's a kind of dumb thing to say."[15]

— RICHARD HAMMING

"It's far better when doing good work is sufficient. In other words, the less attached we are to outcomes the better. When fulfilling our own standards is what fills us with pride and self-respect. When the effort—not the results, good or bad—is enough."[16]

— RYAN HOLIDAY

"Because what I've learned from having the privilege of working in a place that asks for my best and helps me get there is how much it can unlock in a life. The benefits extend far beyond the skills required to get great work done. The really, really good stuff comes from looking back on something you created and thinking, "I had no idea I could do that." It comes from looking around and thinking "wow these people helped me, really helped me, get there." It comes from looking inside and seeing how deep and enduring those feelings of pride, satisfaction, and gratitude really are. And what happens when you have so much it gets to spill over to the other aspects of and people in your life."[17]

— BRIE WOLFSON

ON AMBITION

"That is partly why ambition has become something of a dirty word. We assume that being ambitious means following a pre-written script and climbing a never-ending ladder, sometimes at the expense of other people...

But ambition isn't broken. It is still what it has always been: the innate human desire for growth, a desire that is both universal and highly personal."[18]

— ANNE-LAURE LE CUNFF

EPILOGUE
PARABLE OF THE LAYABOUT AND THE FISHERMAN

Puerto Escondido, Mexico. Two men are on the beach. Carlos, a fisherman, sits at a table. Another man in his late thirties, Luke, sits on the sand writing in his journal.

Carlos puts his beer down after taking a sip. He leans back in his chair and shouts over to Luke, "What's your deal?"

Luke turns and says, "Me? What do you mean?"

"I mean, do you do anything? Like, do you have a job or anything? You've been out here almost every day for three months. Doodling in your notebook."

"I'm retired, actually." Luke keeps writing in his journal.

The fisherman gives Luke a skeptical look, doing a double take, "How? You look like you're in your thirties!" He slowly walks over to Luke's spot on the beach, kneels down beside him, and extends his hand for a handshake.

"Hola, amigo, I'm Carlos." Carlos points far down the

beach to a bunch of boats. "That's mine down there. Been hanging around this beach my whole life."

He turns to Luke, "So what were you saying?"

Luke pauses, his pen hovering over the page. He wonders how much of his story Carlos really wants to hear.

"When I was 23, a couple months into my first job at a big bank, all I could feel was doom. I kept thinking, '*Am I going to do this for the rest of my life?*' Then I stumbled into this online world of early retirement, they call it FIRE, or financially independent, retire early."

Shaking his head, Carlos says, "That's ridiculous."

"Don't have to tell me. Dad thinks I'm nuts. He has a pension, but is still working. He loves work, so maybe that's okay for him. But the summer after I learned about FIRE, I started to plot my escape. And at 34 years old, here I am, retired."

"Doesn't that require making a lot of money?"

"Well, no." Luke flips over to a clean page in his journal and starts jotting down figures. "There's actually this simple formula. For example, if you can save 50% of your salary every year, you can retire in 17 years."

"Seriously?" Carlos takes a seat next to Luke, curious but skeptical.

"The first few years kind of sucked. I wasn't getting paid very much and probably missed out on some of my social life. My first girlfriend dumped me because I refused to go out to eat."

Luke turns to Carlos, who grins.

"That stung." Luke grimaces. "And after that, I decided I needed a little more money. So I taught myself to code by joining a bootcamp, and then shifted to working in tech. The money was insane."

"So then what?"

"Are you sure you want to hear all this? I feel like I must sound like a privileged American."

Carlos laughs and says, "Well, you are. You guys got it good up there for some stuff." He looks out to the water, where several surfers are waiting for the next break.

"But I don't understand your obsession with work. How do people really spend so much time in those office buildings? I grew up on the ocean, I can't imagine not being out here near the water every day. I see all these people who come down here and then work all day, sitting in the cafés in La Punta. What's the point? Gonna save to buy a McMansion back home? You guys got too much stuff."

"Hey man, don't need to convince me." Luke closes his journal and sets it down between him and Carlos.

Carlos chuckles, reflecting on the random conversations he's had with foreigners on the beach over the years. "At least once a year, an over-eager business school student comes down here trying to convince me to turn my boat into a fishing empire. I literally had a Duke Business School student try to convince me to be part of his team's project."

Luke cringes, then shrugs his shoulders. "I used to be like that. I was kind of annoying. I was so obsessed with money, I got really caught up in any money-making venture. I just wanted to escape work. Plus it's hard to not think like that when you grow up in the States. Money is everything there."

The two of them sit quietly for a minute. Luke takes a deep breath and smells the salty air. One of his friends is coming out of the water down the beach and gives him a friendly wave as he walks over to the shower.

Carlos still has questions. He asks again, "Why would you want to retire? Doesn't work bring you some satisfaction?"

"Have you worked in a big corporation?" Luke asks. "It's terrible. Everyone hates it. But no one talks about it. I was one of the few reasonable ones, who actually saw it for what it was, rather than numbing out with alcohol and drugs."

"That happens here, too," Carlos admits with a sigh. "But don't you get bored now that you're not working anymore?"

"Well, that's the thing. I've learned a lot in the past five years since retiring. I used to see work as this awful thing. Something that had to suck. But now, after reading this book *Good Work,* I understand that work can really be anything we are drawn to do. And I'm doing a lot now. I am writing a novel and taking painting classes. I also volunteer as a tutor for an online school. I started dating someone last year and we're going to get married next month and likely start a family."

"Ohhhhh shit, watch out, she's gonna make you get a job!"

Luke smiles. "That would have scared me a few years ago. I was so burned out when I quit. I was terrified to have to go back. But I don't really care if I have to take a job now. I'd do what I need to do for my family. But to be honest, I see so many other ways of making things work before I have to take a job I hate. That's the key thing for me. I just retired from *bad work*."

"I like that idea," says Carlos. "Bad work and good work."

"What about you?" Luke asks. "You seem to be living the dream. You brush off these MBA students and do pretty much what you want. You fish in the morning and hang out here every night with your friends."

"To be honest, I don't love fishing like I used to. Well, I mean, it's fine. Better than an office job for sure! The first twenty years were great. I learned a lot from my father, who was also a fisherman, and I upgraded my boat, helped fund a few other local fishermen over the years and have a small stake in two restaurants. I've actually lived pretty modestly and have some money saved up. So I am in a good position."

"So what's wrong?"

"I don't know. A couple of years ago, I turned 50 and just haven't felt the same since."

"Carlos!" someone yells in the distance. It's his cousin trying to get him to come home for dinner. "Hey," he tells Luke. "I gotta run, see you out here soon?"

"Cool."

A week later, Carlos spots Luke at the beach and walks over to join him. Carlos is carrying two Pacificos.

Making his way across the sand, barefoot, in shorts and no shirt, Carlos waves to Luke.

"Oh hey, haven't seen you the past few days."

"Yeah, we gotta talk, I think you planted some crazy ideas in my head."

"Oh?"

"I've decided to take a year off from fishing."

"Woah, really?" Luke sticks his hand out and accepts the beer from Carlos, taking a sip and then putting it down in the sand.

Carlos continues, "Yeah, you inspired me. You seem so alive with energy and I've been thinking about how I just don't get what I once used to from fishing. Oh, and since we talked on Tuesday I can't stop thinking about the dream I once had to live on my sailboat for a year."

"So you're going to sail around the world?"

"Well, I don't know how far I'll get, but that's the idea. My nephew is bugging me to give him more freedom to take over the boat and fishing enterprise anyway. I took over when I was 23, and he's already 30. Maybe it's time to pass the torch."

"That sounds like a solid plan."

"Yeah, but it's scary. How do you actually do something bold like this?"

Luke closes his eyes, takes a deep breath, and exhales. "I wish I had left earlier. I mean, I'm glad I was able to save money and 'retire,' but I actually feel like I wasted most of those ten years doing things I didn't love and living life by the numbers on a spreadsheet. I ignored my inner ambitions for years." Luke turns to look at Carlos. "Like your sailing trip."

Suddenly Carlos has more questions. "What would you do differently if you could go back?"

"Well," Luke reflects, "I think I was right about working for a big company. It did suck. Everyone complained about it all the time. But I underestimated how much time it would take me to recover after I quit. In the first few years, I floundered. I didn't know how to lean into doing new things without feeling like a fraud. Now it feels like I'm just getting started with my life. It's really sad. I don't know where the writing and painting will take me, but it feels like something I can actually commit to for the rest of my life. And that gives me hope."

"Wow, that's powerful."

"Yeah. Do you think you can fish for the rest of your life?"

Carlos finishes his beer and puts the bottle down next to Luke's. "Probably not. My heart's not in it anymore. But deep down, I know there's this fire still burning in me. My adventurous spirit. I guess I'm also a bit nervous that the sailing trip will not be what I want."

Luke raises his eyebrows. "But what if it is?"

Carlos scans the horizon, feeling a mix of anxiety and excitement brewing within him. *Could he really do this?* His father's legacy, the boat, the local community that saw him a certain way – could he walk away?

Luke notices Carlos' discomfort. "You know, doing this might be the most ambitious thing you can do."

Carlos nods and smiles as relief washes over his body.

"Ambitious? Huh."

He had never thought about this choice as ambitious. Instead, he thought he was abandoning everything. He had just met Luke this week, but for the first time in a long time, he felt understood. He couldn't explain it, but having this random person believe in him gave him the sense that he was enough.

He didn't know how his extended family would take it, but for the first time in a long time, he felt something inside of him coming alive. Something that was going to set him adrift...

ACKNOWLEDGMENTS

It's quite the feeling to finish another book. About a year ago, I had no idea if it would be possible.

At the time, I was deep in the draft of another book I had started. I ended up writing about 55,000 words in that draft. But the more I wrote, the more convoluted it became.

In writing this book, I realized that I had lost connection to writing. For five years prior to having a child, I enjoyed an effortless connection with writing, from that moment in Taipei. I really didn't need to think about how to make writing happen. It just happened.

While I enjoyed being a dad far more than I ever expected, trying to casually fit writing around the edges of the new life phases I stepped into seemed to be much harder than I expected.

Through this book, I was able to find my way back to that sense of connection with my work.

None of this would have been possible without friends and family and fans rooting me on.

Most important of those people is Angie.

You are my superpower. From the beginning of our relationship, you've had 100% faith in me to figure everything out. It scares me how much you believe in me but it also pushes me to be wildly ambitious about the life we are building. Having you in my corner feels like cheating. So thank you Angie for your relentless support.

In addition, I want to thank many people:

Jonny Miller for being a good friend on this weird journey for more than six years now and happening to be there at the start of both books. Kelly Wilde-Miller and Adam Spooner for that magical lunch overlooking the mountains. Something special clicked for me those few days and this book wouldn't have happened without it.

Nat Eliason, Nathan Baugh, Noah Huisman, and Billy Oppenheimer for the co-writing sessions and nerdy conversations about writing. You help me feel normal for being so obsessed with writing.

To many Austin friends, who have helped me feel comfortable stepping into my own inner ambition over the last few years especially Sky King and Alex Hardy.

And to the many others that have supported me and inspired me in countless ways: Scott Britton, Tommy Lee, Cam Houser, David Perell, Michelle Varghese, Andrew Voshage, Anne-Laure Le Cunff, Nick Gray, Khe Hy, Danny Miranda, Kevin Shen, Kevin Dahlstrom, Michael Ashcroft, Tom Critchlow, Jordan Litner, Andrew Kappel, and Jeremy Finch.

Thank you to the many creative people who influenced this book:

Paula Trucks-Pape, for valuable editing, coaching, and general support as we have finished our second book together! Melina Burhan for the beautiful illustrations. Garrett Kincaid for the developmental coaching and last-minute feedback. Lydia Chen, Michael Dean, Calvin Rosser, Alex Dobrenko, and Valerie Zhang for valuable feedback on versions of this book. And Nate Kadlac and Eli Schiff for the design counsel and support.

Finally, to my family:

Mom and dad for giving my a strong foundation to follow my dreams. To my aunts Denise, Debbie, and Diana - thank you for your support and being original "pathless" role models balancing careers and parenting before it was cool. To my uncles: David, Tom, and Andy, mostly because I know you'll give me a hard time if I mention the aunts and not you.

Pursuing ambitious goals, like writing a book, can be daunting—even for those with an established audience. Luckily, I have people rooting for me and a support network that gives my courage. For this, I'm profoundly grateful.

Yet I'm not alone in chasing bold dreams. Countless others are stepping out of their comfort zones, daring to search for their good work, and doing things that are scary. We need more of this and I'd encourage you to root for these people in your life.

ABOUT THE AUTHOR
PAUL MILLERD

Paul Millerd is an independent writer, freelancer, coach, and digital creator. He has written online for many years and has built a growing audience of curious humans from around the world. His first book, The Pathless Path, has sold 50k+ books worldwide and is being translated into several languages. Before finding his good work, he spent several years doing strategy consulting and operations work for big companies. He is fascinated about how our relationship to work is shifting and how more people can live lives where they can thrive.

For more: pmillerd.com

ALSO BY PAUL MILLERD

The Pathless Path, Published January 2022.
To read the introduction for free: pathlesspath.com

NOTES

PART ONE QUOTES

1. Palmer, P. J. (2015). Let your life speak: Listening for the Voice of Vocation. John Wiley & Sons.
2. Varty, B. (2019). *The Lion Tracker's guide to life*. HarperCollins.
3. Whyte, David. *Crossing the Unknown Sea: Work as a Pilgrimage of Identity*. Penguin, 2002.

2. FOLLOW YOUR ENERGY

1. Derek Sivers, Hell yeah or no (2020), https://sive.rs/n

3. COMMIT TO THE JOURNEY

1. Ben Katt, The Way Home: Discovering the Hero's Journey to Wholeness at Midlife, St. Martin's Essentials, 2024.
2. Lubas, Caitlyn. "Chapter 30: Lessons From Life on a Remote Island." You Are Where You Go, 7 Aug. 2024, open.substack.com/pub/youarewhereyougo/p/chapter-30-lessons-from-life-on-a?r=700d&utm_campaign=post&utm_medium=web.
3. Cécile Marion, "8 months into my sabbatical," (n.d.), https://www.cecilemarion.org/post/following-the-inscrutable-exhortations-of-my-soul
4. V, Samantha. "185. We Are Never Going Back to Work." Build A Wealthy Spirit Podcast, 6 Aug. 2024, www.buildawealthyspirit.com/p/185-we-are-never-going-back-to-work?r=700d&utm_campaign=post&utm_medium=web.

PART TWO QUOTES

1. Jobs, Steve. *Make Something Wonderful: Steve Jobs in His Own Words*. 2023.

2. Vonnegut, Kurt. *How to Write With Style*. 1980.

5. FIND A POSITIVE EDGE

1. Robert Frost - A Servant to Servants. (n.d.). https://www.poetry verse.com/robert-frost-poems/a-servant-to-servants
2. Patrick O'Shaughnessy, social media post, 22 Nov. 2023, https://x.com/patrick_oshag/status/1727340286982967711

6. DON'T MISTAKE A GOOD JOB FOR GOOD WORK

1. Byung-Chul Han. The Burnout Society. Stanford UP, 2015.
2. By all means, go ahead and share this book as wide and far as you wish. We can make this "books to bricks" fairytale come true!
3. Paul Millerd, The Pathless Path: Imagining a New Story for Work and Life, 2022.

7. QUESTION YOUR WORK SCRIPTS

1. Emily Stewart, "Useless Jobs and Getting Away With Doing Nothing at Work," Vox, 24 May 2023, www.vox.com/money/23733244/bullshit-jobs-work-employment-lazy-jobless-employed-nothing-to-do
2. N. Malone, "The age of anti ambition," The New York Times, 15 February 2022
3. Luke Burgis, "How to know what you really want," Big Think, 15 November 2021, https://bigthink.com/series/explain-it-like-im-smart/mimetic-desires/
4. "Arjun Khemani — the Hunt for Better Problems (EP. 213)." *Apple Podcasts*, interview by Jim O'Shaughnessy, 25 Apr. 2024, podcasts.apple.com/us/podcast/arjun-khemani-the-hunt-for-better-problems-ep-213/id1489171190?i=1000653540630

PART THREE QUOTES

1. Working It Out: 23 Women Writers, Artists, Scientists, and Scholars Talk About Their Lives and Work: Virginia Valiant, et. al:

9780394409368: Amazon.com: Books. www.amazon.com/Working-Out-Writers-Scientists-Scholars/dp/0394409361.

2. Whyte, David. *Crossing the Unknown Sea: Work as a Pilgrimage of Identity*. Penguin, 2002.

8. SOLVE THE PUZZLE OF GOOD WORK

1. L. Fadulu, "How Philip Glass went from driving taxis to composing." The Atlantic, 27 February 2019, https://www.theatlantic.com/business/archive/2018/04/philip-glass-taxi-driver-composer/558278/

2. D. Perell, "Addicted to Distraction - Ted Gioia," How I Write Podcast, 29 May 2024, https://podcasts.apple.com/gb/podcast/addicted-to-distraction-ted-gioia-how-i-write-podcast/id1700171470?i=1000657150661

3. R. Lewis, "Why you should start living in the past," Honestly Human 9 May 2024, https://www.pivottothepodium.com/p/why-you-should-start-living-in-the?r=700d&utm_campaign=post&utm_medium=web

9. DO WHAT FEELS RIGHT

1. "The Opposite of Trying." *Art of Accomplishment*, 17 Mar. 2023, www.artofaccomplishment.com/podcast/the-opposite-of-trying.

10. FIND THE ZEAL

1. Noah Huisman, "On Sloth," 18 March 2024, https://noahhuisman.substack.com/p/on-sloth

2. Jensen Huang, Keynote address, Stanford Institute for Economic Policy Research (SIEPR) Economic Summit, 7 March 2024,.https://www.youtube.com/watch?v=cEg8cOx7UZk

3. Eric S. Yuan. What I Learned From Jensen Huang, CEO of NVIDIA. 22 Oct. 2020, www.linkedin.com/pulse/what-i-learned-from-jensen-huang-ceo-nvidia-eric-s-yuan.

4. Gorlin, Gena. "Embracing Healthy Ambition | Q&A With Gena Gorlin | #269." Pathless by Paul Millerd, 22 June 2024, newsletter.-

pathlesspath.com/p/embracing-health-ambition-q-and-a?
r=7ood&utm_campaign=post&utm_medium=web.

11. SEE YOUR WORK AS IT IS

1. W. T. Gallwey, The inner game of tennis, 1974
2. Gallwey, Inner game
3. W. T. Gallwey, The inner game of tennis, 1974
4. Andrew Taggart, "Silicon Valley Wants to Sell Us Solutions—but Are We Sure There's a Problem in the First Place?" Quartz, 20 July 2022, qz.com/1065179/silicon-valley-wants-to-sell-us-solutions-but-are-we-sure-theres-a-problem-in-the-first-place.

PART FOUR QUOTES

1. Gilbert, Elizabeth. *Big Magic: How to Live a Creative Life, and Let Go of Your Fear*. Bloomsbury Publishing, 2015.
2. Lee, Min Jin. *Free Food for Millionaires*. Random House, 2012.

12. LEAVE MONEY ON THE TABLE

1. Paul Millerd, The ten most surprising benefits of self-employment, blog post, 28 March 2024,,. https://pmillerd.com/the-ten-most-surprising-benefits-of-self-employment/
2. Paul Millerd, "The money path or the life path? - Tim Malnick," The Pathless Path Podcast, 28 March 2022, https://podcasts.apple.com/dk/podcast/the-money-path-or-the-life-path-tim-malnick/id1328600107?i=1000555526877
3. Ali Abdaal. (2023, December 8). "Everything's changing - Life update," 8 December 2023, https://www.youtube.com/watch?v=XtOshDbMGkA. You can also find April Perry's work at: https://learndobecome.com/about/

QUOTES THAT INSPIRED THIS BOOK

1. Palmer, P. J. (2015). Let your life speak: Listening for the Voice of Vocation. John Wiley & Sons.

2. Crawford, M. B. (2009). Shop Class as Soulcraft: An Inquiry Into the Value of Work. Penguin.

3. Fromm, E. (1956). *The art of loving.* https://ci.nii.ac.jp/ncid/BA85629792

4. Soros, George. *Soros on Soros: Staying Ahead of the Curve.* John Wiley and Sons, 1995.

5. *Working It Out: 23 Women Writers, Artists, Scientists, and Scholars Talk About Their Lives and Work: Virginia Valiant, et. al: 9780394409368: Amazon.com: Books.* www.amazon.com/Working-Out-Writers-Scientists-Scholars/dp/0394409361.

6. Ogilvy, D. M. (1995). The unpublished David Ogilvy.

7. Jobs, S. (2023). Make something wonderful: Steve Jobs in His Own Words.

8. D. Perell, "How writing helped Jason Fried build an 8-Figure business," How I Write Podcast, 22 May 2024, https://podcasts.apple.com/gb/podcast/how-writing-helped-jason-fried-build-an-8-figure-business/id1700171470?i=1000656378679

9. Iyer, Pico. *The Art of Stillness: Adventures in Going Nowhere.* Simon and Schuster, 2014.

10. Moss, Adam. *The Work of Art: How Something Comes from Nothing.* Penguin, 2024.

11. Whyte, David. *Crossing the Unknown Sea: Work as a Pilgrimage of Identity.* Penguin, 2002.

12. Berry, W. (2015). *The Unsettling of America: Culture & Agriculture.* Catapult.

13. Gilbert, E. (2015). Big magic: How to Live a Creative Life, and Let Go of Your Fear. Bloomsbury Publishing.

14. Carlyle, Thomas. *Past and Present.* Oxford UP, 2023.

15. Hamming, R. W. (2020). *The art of doing science and engineering: Learning to Learn.* Stripe Press.

16. Holiday, Ryan. *Ego Is the Enemy.* Penguin, 2016.

17. Wolfson, Brie. *What I Miss About Working at Stripe.* 9 Sept. 2024, every.to/p/what-i-miss-about-working-at-stripe?sid=15169.

18. Cunff, Anne-Laure Le. *Tiny Experiments: How to Live Freely in a Goal-Obsessed World.* Penguin Group, 2025.

LIVE FULLY NOW

1. T&H - Inspiration & Motivation. "Live Fully Now - Alan Watts." *YouTube*, 14 Apr. 2014, www.youtube.com/watch?v=HdqVF7-8wng.

Live Fully Now

My goodness, don't you remember when you went first to school. You went to kindergarten, and in kindergarten, the idea was to push along so that you could get into first grade.

And then push along so that you could get into second grade, third grade, and so on, going up and up. And then you went to high school and this was a great transition in life.

Now the pressure is being put on, you must get ahead. You must go up the grades and finally be good enough to get to college.

And then when you get to college, you're still going step by step...up to the great moment in which you're ready to go out into the world.

Then when you get out into this famous world, comes the struggle for success in profession or business. And again, there seems to be a ladder before you, something for which you're reaching for all the time.

And then, suddenly, when you're about 40 or 45 years old, in the middle of life, you wake up one day and say "huh? I've arrived and, by Joe, I feel pretty much the same as I've always felt. In fact I'm not so sure that I don't feel a little bit cheated." Because, you see, you were fooled. You were always living for somewhere where you aren't.

And while, as I said, it is of tremendous use for us to be able to look ahead in this way and to plan. There is no use in planning for a future, which when you get to it and it becomes the present you won't be there.

You'll be living in some other future which hasn't yet arrived.

And so in this way, one is never able actually to inherit and enjoy the fruits of one's actions.

You can't live it all unless you can live fully now.[1]

— ALAN WATTS

Made in the USA
Las Vegas, NV
25 September 2024